LESSONS FROM MY COACH

Become an **Extraordinary** Coach
Attract **Extraordinary** Clients

AMIR KARKOUTI

Author of **Do Nothing to Get Everything**

LESSONS FROM MY COACH
Become and Extraordinary Coach
Attract Extraordinary Clients

ISBN 13: 978-1-93974-502-6
ISBN 10: 1-93974-502-0

Library of Congress Control Number: 2014932052

Printed in the United States of America

Published by Old University Press

www.amirkarkouti.com

To my Coach, Rich Litvin
The person who showed me what it means
to be a transformative coach.

To Holly Karkouti
My Love and ultimate "life" coach

Contents

FOREWORD

The Ordinary Behind the Extraordinary

As I listened to Amir Karkouti share the story of his early life, tears began to run down my face. You see, I'd admired Amir for his skills as an entrepreneur and the fact that he'd published three books and that he was a charismatic speaker on stage. But what I hadn't realized is just what it took to create all these successes in his life.

Amir described to me how his mother and father had fled the trauma of the revolution in Tehran in search of a better life. With two young boys—Amir and his brother—they traveled, worked, and lived in Germany, Turkey, and across the United States. Life was really challenging for them and like many immigrant families they survived on little—government assistance and a range of cramped, one-bedroom apartments. As a young boy, he'd regularly have to say goodbye to his father—not knowing if he'd ever see him again—as his dad risked his life on a regular basis to return to his hometown to bring support to his own extended family. I'm a new dad and imagining what this family went through—and what Amir went through in his formative years—really moved me.

Fear, Insecurity, and Lack of Belief

Fear, insecurity, and lack of belief were constant companions in Amir's early life, even as—ever so slowly—his family inched their way up to a more comfortable lifestyle.

That didn't make things any easier for Amir, though. English was his third language and his teachers were convinced he would always have trouble communicating and expressing himself to others. Can you imagine how it felt to a little kid, trying his very best, when his junior high teachers told him that he would have trouble understanding and learning the English language for the rest of his life?

With a sense of determination and fueled by a desire to

succeed, despite the odds Amir eventually became the chief financial officer of a restaurant chain that he still runs. He lacked even a college degree, but that couldn't stop him from helping the business open seven restaurants. The problem was that underneath it all, every decision he made was still from fear and distress. He almost went bankrupt and in the process he lost his house, had to sell his car, and started again completely from scratch.

The 100% Rule

What moves me most about Amir's story is that he has been clear since he was a young boy that he will never let circumstances define him. He's now the author of three books, an accomplished public speaker, and just recently his restaurant—with no marketing, coupons, or special offers—won San Diego's A-list out of 53 other restaurants.

Here's one of the unorthodox secrets to his business success—every new member of staff is trained in Amir's 100% Rule:

> Part 1 of the 100% Rule says: When you go to work you do everything with 100% love, 100% service, and 100% devotion and presence to staff and guests. You don't bring in family problems, money issues, rumors or gossip.

> Part 2 of the 100% Rule says: When you go home you do everything with 100% love, 100% service, and 100% devotion and presence to your partner and your kids. You don't bring in work problems, money issues, rumors or gossip.

Stop Thinking

The English term "coach" is derived from a Hungarian word meaning "carriage," and it's an apt metaphor because far too often in life we get *carried away* with our thinking.

Socrates once said, "I cannot teach anybody anything. I can only make them think." Well, the role of a coach is actually quite the reverse. You cannot teach anybody anything. You can only help them to *stop* thinking—for a moment. And in-between their thoughts lie life-changing insights.

Spend time with an extraordinary coach and your thinking will slow down enough for such insights. Spend time with an extraordinary coach and you'll find a way to turn each insight into specific actions. Take action on your deepest wisdom and you will truly transform your life.

Amir is one of those extraordinary coaches.

If you are a coach, it's time to stop thinking for a moment.

And whilst you do, take a moment to read this book.

It may just change your life.

But only if you *apply* what you learn.

Rich Litvin, Los Angeles, November 2013
Founder of the High-Achieving Introvert Project
Founder of The Confident Woman's Salon
Co-author of The Prosperous Coach
www.RichLitvin.com

When you get free from certain fixed concepts of the way the world is, you find it is far more subtle, and far more miraculous, than you thought it was.

— Alan Watts

INTRODUCTION
What You're Reading May Change Your Life

That's a bold statement to be making. Not many books have started an introduction with such a statement. The good news is, it's not the book that will change your life; it's the actions you take from just a single idea in the book. How can I make such a claim? Because my coach, Rich Litvin, showed me how this is possible.

Let's go back to my first conversation with Rich. I saw Rich coach in a seminar and he turned my life around. He said just one sentence, which I will divulge in the next few chapters, that changed my life. I was a struggling coach, trying to make it in a field that is often misunderstood. I knew what I had to offer the world was extremely powerful and life changing. The problem wasn't what I knew, the problem was that I was afraid. I was using marketing methods and I was given the wrong idea about how to get extraordinary clients.

After the seminar, I jumped into my car in Los Angeles and zipped home to San Diego and completely changed my website, got rid of my business cards, and went out into the world to coach. I felt like I had started all over again. In a way, it was starting anew.

One day out of the blue, Rich called me to personally invite me to a seminar he was running in Los Angeles. He told me that he was going to fill up his seminar one person at a time by calling people and telling them what the seminar was about. I thought that was cool, and a neat marketing trick.

Later, I'd find out it wasn't a trick at all. It's how he serves his clients, makes sure that every person attending will get value, and that the people attending are the type of people he wants at his events. With no Facebook, Twitter, landing page, or video, he filled up a room with coaches, one person at a time.

When he called me, I was on a different path. I was tech savvy, an Internet marketer, and I was going to get my clients via videos, credentials, and sending out as many postcards, ads, and whatever else I could do to build my clientele.

At one point during our conversation, after he invited me to the seminar, he asked me if he could support me with anything at the moment. I said yes. I told him that I had recently written a book called *Do NOTHING to Get EVERYTHING*, which is my manifesto for well-being, and that I wanted to be a number-one Amazon bestseller. I told him that I'd found a guy who could shoot me up through the charts, and that he could get a big list of followers to buy my book and create a campaign. It was going to be huge!

He apologized and told me that he wasn't interested in helping me achieve that status.

I have to be honest. I was a bit pissed off and confused. So, I paused for a minute and said to him, "I don't think you understand, Rich. Once I become an Amazon bestseller, I'll have better credentials and people will know who I am."

After his trademark silence, he finally asked me, "So, what is it that you are trying to accomplish by becoming an Amazon bestseller?"

Agitated, I said, "So I can help people."

He paused again, and this time his pause was twice as long as the first. The pause allowed my mind to settle back to the speed of life. Then he said, "Do you know what the best way is to help someone? It's by helping them! Your credentials aren't going to help them; your Amazon status isn't going to help them. You coaching people is going to help them."

I was ready to spend three months creating a campaign to prove to people that I was a worthy coach, and that all went down the drain with one profound statement.

If everything I am doing is meant to have the result of helping people, why don't I shortcut all of the fluff in-between and simply...HELP PEOPLE!

My bank account was a perfect confirmation that whatever I was doing wasn't working. After our conversation, Rich invited me to a two-hour coaching session at the SLS Hotel, and my life expanded even more. He showed me exactly how to coach clients and be compensated for it.

I made more money by that one insight he'd given me than from any Internet marketing seminar, list-building tactic, or credential-building trick I'd tried in the past.

Why?

Because marketing tactics, list building, or credential approval is not appropriate if you want to be an extraordinary coach. Like many in our field, I was fooled and dumbfounded. It was right in front of me, but I didn't see it all along. It took only one insight to change all of that.

I ended up hiring Rich to coach me, and each phone call and email exchange we had opened my eyes even more. The simplicity of serving the person in front of you and making money as a side-effect of serving was astonishing. I couldn't believe how easy it was. Having a successful coach and taking action from each coaching session was all it took to change my coaching profession. I became my own guinea pig to see if five years of traditional list building, marketing, and mass mailers was going to be debunked by the simple idea of serving the person in front of me.

I played 100% full-out, and listened to my coach. I wanted to see what could happen. My world was transformed, and along the way, I took notes for myself as I was cruising through the insights and new understandings I had received.

So, here you are, reading this book. This book is all the ideas I have received from Rich and the other coaches in my life who have changed the road to my success. I have realized that my biggest life turns and breakthroughs were made by single insights that I turned into actions.

That's it.

As a coach, if you can open the way to have your clients see one insight and take action on it, their lives will change. With that being said, I hope you get one insight from this book, like my coaches have gifted to me, to move you to a world that you never thought possible.

My coaches have changed my life. They gave me the space and momentum to create miracles. It is now my job to run with those miracles and turn them into reality. My goal is to do the same for you—to open up that space where you are willing to go against the status quo, be open to another way to coach, and get extraordinary clients in your life.

You are not going to find marketing tactics, list building, or bullet-point lists of secrets in my book, as in so many other fly-by-night books on marketing or coaching. This book is different. This book is to be read like you are ready for a transformation. All the insights that made it into this book were handpicked because they either changed my life, or the lives of my clients or other coaches. It's that powerful.

Ultimately, you will be the person to decide what you get out of the chapters. YOU will have to create the "meat" of the success by the insights you get from the book. No two coaches will read this book the same way and no two coaches will succeed the same way.

One thing I am sure of: If you follow and act upon one single insight, you will drastically change your coaching. Coaching is a very intimate profession, and most books on marketing your practice or handling clients are just not fit for extraordinary coaches working with extraordinary clients.

This book is written for coaches who want to move their clients to a better place. It's written to make you a better coach and offer a new way for you to get extraordinary clients. My coaches have done this for me, and now it's my turn to pay it forward to all the extraordinary coaches who are reading this book.

Chapter 1
Nurturing Your Insights

Nobody has the power to take two steps together; you can take only one step at a time.
Osho

I wish somebody had told me this before. This is the secret that has been missing in all the books I've read on becoming a better person, of knowing who you are, and achieving your dreams.

We live in a time where we can get lightning-fast information at any moment. Want to know the weather? Check your phone. See what's going on eight months from now? Check your calendar that's linked to your iPad. There is some value to this fast-paced world we live in, but there is also tremendous value in the cultivation of the other part of our brain that doesn't work on speed. The other part works on the nurturing and slowing down of life. This part of the brain is the part that doesn't have rhyme or reason for an insight that pops up; those brilliant "aha!" moments that you surely couldn't come up with on your own...but somehow, by some sheer miracle, did.

It's the ONE insight we get.

But in our speedy world, we see an insight fly past us so quickly we miss its gifts. We miss tremendous gifts. Some can be life changing. Some are so powerful that they can save a life. I know this for a fact. I've had a life-changing moment with a client who was ready to kill himself. But ONE insight changed his life.

He was ready to kill himself. I asked him how he knew. He told me because the voice in his head told him to. I asked him if he would do it if I told him to. He said, "No." Then I asked him why he thought the voices in his head were more important than my voice. He cried and got an insight. He realized that he didn't have to act on what every voice in his head said.

We sat in silence. He wept.

ONE INSIGHT changed everything. It changed his world view.

One insight saved his life. He was smart enough to run with that one insight. He didn't need any more than that one insight to shift his world view. He saw the value in sitting in one insight. If he had just brushed off that one insight and looked for a bigger one, who knows where his life might have been today...

There is so much gold in one insight that we may miss it.

Again...

There is SO MUCH GOLD in ONE INSIGHT that we may miss it!

Before we go deeper, what is an insight?

In-Sight

1. the ability to perceive clearly or deeply; penetration

2. a penetrating and often sudden understanding, as of a complex situation or problem

3. (Psychology) *Psychol*

a. the capacity for understanding one's own or another's mental processes

b. the immediate understanding of the significance of an event or action

An insight is a game changer. An insight turns your world around from what may have seemed impossible mere seconds ago. Insights are the wipers of our souls. They clean away the gunk that hides our true nature so we can see what we've been missing.

Look back at your life and remember a turning point. Remember that moment when it just came to you out of nowhere? Think of the moment when your body flushed with energy—this electric energy out of nowhere. We get insights from everywhere. Good times, bad times, before we go to sleep, on our way to work. We get insights when we should be paying attention to something, or paying our bills.

But here is the tricky part. Insights are worthless if they are not nurtured. I remember having a coaching call with my coach, Rich Litvin, and I asked him a question. His answer was so amazing that I was ready for 10 more insights so I could have my "money's worth" on the call. He knew better. I was ready to disrespect the power of ONE INSIGHT.

As soon as I had the "aha" moment I was ready to jump to another. He stopped me dead in my tracks and said, "Let's go back to your question and dig deeper." He asked me, "What was that aha for?" He knew he had found gold.

The rest of the call was nothing more but solidifying that one insight. He wanted to mold that insight and grow it; make it move, get bigger, and transfer to physical reality.

What does the insight mean in my life NOW?

How does the ONE insight CHANGE EVERYTHING?

One of our calls lasted only 15 minutes. He didn't care to use the hour because he knew I'd run with the insight. I was starting to get the idea. Unlike some things in our lives, insights are not quantity based. It's not about how many you can hold in a basket. When we slow down to see the ONE insight that we get, it's time to become a gardener.

But before you can become a gardener, fence that insight in and make sure to protect it. Protect it from the naysayers, and the fast-paced life that tells you to look for something bigger and better. Protect it from yourself, who wants to speed up to find the next big insight. Put a fence around it so you can sit in that moment when you get a feeling and when you know that your ENTIRE WORLD, your innermost being, has just changed.

Then, in your mind, walk over to that garden, close the gate behind you, and sit with that insight. It's time to cultivate it.

When we get the shift from one insight, and the surge of energy of what possibilities are now in front of us, it may seem natural to utilize that burst of energy to gain more insights. Don't go there just yet. Dig deeper with the insight. It's like getting a hit of speed. We want to smack our veins again to get more. Don't do it. Feel the insight and what it means.

YOUR WORLD HAS CHANGED.

You are not in the same womb as you were in the last world you were living in before the insight. Give the insight some breathing room. Slowly wake it up and nurture it. Look at the new world you live in now with the insight that just came in. Look around you and see what actions you can take NOW. What would keep the momentum of that one insight going? Dig deeper.

You may get "mini-insights" and bursts of energy when you are following that one insight. Stick with it. Don't forget the first "aha."

In my profession, people think my job is to give them one to two hours of brilliant advice, suggestions, or ideas. As a coach, I am supposed to give my clients information they may not have had before. Nonsense. My job is to open up space for my client to have ONE insight! Then, like a stopped heart that's been jump-started...slow it down to beat normally again. Slow it down so life catches up and they can use their insight today, in this moment. Create actionable steps where their insight will carry them into the new world it created.

My job is not to give them the rest of the hour. Insights don't go by a preset time. My job is to get off the phone or end the meeting to let them ride the true potential of that one insight.

Don't dismiss the power of that one insight. It's that powerful. This is what Steve Chandler, another brilliant coach, says is the difference between information vs. transformation.

If you got an insight from reading this...STOP READING NOW and start cultivating that insight. Move with it and see what it's supposed to do for you.

If you haven't gotten one yet...there is nothing to do. When one comes, jump right in. Your world will change.

It only takes one INSIGHT.

Chapter 2
Slow Down...

*Slow down and everything you are chasing will
come around and catch you.*
John De Paola

This was a tough one for me. This one is also a tough one for my clients. This one is the brains behind the insights in the last chapter. Without slowing down, the insights just zip away. Gone.

I remember when I hired my coach. I wanted him to tell me his secrets. I wanted to know what he did on stage that was so awe-inspiring and made everyone in the room feel the transformation.

I wanted to know. I was ready for him to give me the *Cliff Notes* and get on with it. On our first call he could tell I was excited. He could tell I was ready to move, make some changes in my world. I was. I wanted to know the secrets so I could hang up and start utilizing them with my clients. So the call began.

I started rambling and he figured it out. He let me finish my rambling and he asked me after a long pause..."What would make this call powerful for you?"

My head was spinning and now I was frustrated. Hadn't he heard all the stuff I was telling him? He had, but that was not what he had asked me.

He paused for a minute. I knew he was still on the line. He let my thoughts settle and from dead silence his voice emerged again. "Amir, what would make this call powerful for you?"

I felt like my dad had taken the candy out of my hands so I would pay attention. He slowed me down so much that I started

6

to *feel* my conversation. I was going at the pace where my life and my thoughts were on the same page. I stopped and sat with him in silence. Then I asked him, "What is the most important thing for me to know to be a better coach?"

He told me to slow down...slow down so much that your life speeds up. Slow down to a point where you feel where you are in this very moment. Slow down to be present enough to connect with your client.

After 11 years of learning everything I could about self-development and psychology, he wanted me to slow down. Why? Because the answers aren't in the information. The answers are in the pockets of insights that arise when your mind is still. Insights and answers show up when your brain decides to believe you, now that you're not busy.

It reminds me of a story Supercoach Michael Neill once told. He was telling his audience to imagine that you are at a bus stop and every bus that passes by is an insight. Imagine there is a person next to you who is frazzled and talking your ear off, telling everyone that he keeps missing the bus. And as he keeps talking, his attention is away from all the buses (insights) that keep passing him by and he thinks that jabbering away will somehow relieve his situation. What if you told him to slow down for a minute and stop talking? Just sit on the bench and look up. How much more would you have to do at that point? How many buses (insights) would be traveling past, and how many of them would he finally see?

It's not by speeding up our lives that we go through them fully and immersed. It's always by slowing down. One insight at a time.

I was taken by surprise when I realized what my coach Rich had done that day when I saw him on stage. It wasn't a tool, trick, or technique. He just slowed down the conversation. He would sit in silence until the words he needed to say came out. Like a skilled surgeon, every word, every sentence, carved out a slice of self-doubt, worry, or self-illusion.

We forget that nothingness in a song is just as important as the notes in-between. If we speed up a song, it won't have the same sound. It would feel rushed and it would just be noise, scrambled, jumbled, and out of tune. That also holds true for our life tune. Enjoy the pauses. Find the power in them. Slow down the conversation to one insight. Don't allow yourself or your clients to jump around with their questions like it's a competition. Stop the conversation mid-sentence if you see that they are spinning and running nowhere. Stop them, sit in silence, and ask them once again (when they are listening)...

"What would make this a powerful conversation for you?"

Watch the magic unfold.

Chapter 3
Know Less Than Your Clients

The only true wisdom is in knowing you know nothing.
Socrates

I would prepare for days before my sessions with my clients. I would send them a questionnaire that was 10 pages long and have them answer questions that made the paper more of an interrogation piece than a helpful information packet.

I thought I had to do that. I was scared.

What if I missed something and they caught me? What if I showed up and they knew more than me? What if they started asking me questions and I wasn't prepared?

I didn't look forward to a lot of my client sessions. Can you blame me? I have heard this and similar issues with a lot of people in the helping professions. Go to any bookstore and you'll see aisles and aisles of books telling you about every technique that will work on clients. There are books that teach you 1001 questions to ask your clients. There are books that teach you the right way to get someone out of misery, emotional pain, and trauma. So much to digest and remember.

But my coach taught me something that changed all of that. I had asked him what questions I should ask. What would make the coaching impactful for my clients? The most important questions I wanted answered were: How will they know that I can help them? How can I prove my worthiness as a coach?

His answer was simple. Know *less* than your client. The whole time I'd been getting coached, I'd been waiting for him to give me crazy advice and insights only a coach would have. Nope. He'd just ask questions and provide a few powerful stories in-between.

But the stories would not show up until the questions were asked. He would ask what would make this conversation a miracle or powerful. He would ask why that's important. And would then...wait.

Then he would ask me if I'd be open to going deeper into the question. Then he would wait. And ask another question. He didn't have the answers I was looking for. He knew that all along. He knew that *I had the answers I was looking for*. I was just asking myself the wrong questions. So, he showed up empty. He showed up and sat empty and asked questions. One question led to another. Space would open and an insight would form. The insights lay somewhere between the empty space and the question.

That was such a breakthrough for me. I didn't have to know more than my client. I had to know how to find out what my clients wanted, and the only way to find out was to ask questions. Simple ones. I had to really dig deep to see if what they were asking was really what they wanted.

Want to find out how? Ask them if that's what they really want. Keep digging and you'll both feel the air shift when something clicks. Don't rush to the next question. See if the first question was completely answered. Find the art in *seeking*. It's more important than any trick, tool, or technique you've been taught.

Want to know how to start? Ask your client: What would make this conversation a game changer, powerful, amazing or a miracle? Sit and listen. The magic will unfold with your patience and open heart. The rest is easy.

High-touch vs high-tech: In a high-tech world that is growing exponentially, the real competitive advantage you have as a coach is to go high-touch. You can't outpace technology: Facebook, Twitter, Pinterest, LinkedIn, Google+, Snapchat, Instagram, Vine, YouTube, blogging, infographics, email, apps, SEO, internet marketing, podcasts, hashtags...

What did I miss? Who cares?

Reach out to someone. Serve them, help them, love them, appreciate them, acknowledge them, challenge them.
— Rich Litvin

Chapter 4
The Coaching Starts NOW

*Do not wait until the conditions are perfect to begin. Beginning
makes the conditions perfect.*

Alan Cohen

I remember getting into a conversation about marriage with
my best friend. We had a bit of a disagreement about the
value of a wedding. He told me that a wedding was what
changed everything for him. I told him that my marriage had
already started, when I first laid eyes on her. In other words, the
way you show up in the world—whether it's in your relationships,
work, family life, etc.—is how you will always behave. The raise at
work, the marriage certificate when you're married, or the ticket
you get from the police will not change that.

So, I told my friend that the marriage starts NOW. I had
already paved the way to our marriage and anything in-between
was going to be beautiful events showcasing our love. With that
being said, the same goes for coaching.

I have seen so many coaches tell their clients that once they
sign up, they'll tell them what they need to do. I have witnessed
coaches telling me that they will keep their best coaching advice
to themselves until the client pays. Why? I'm not sure. But I'll tell
you that my coaching always starts NOW, from the moment I
meet a client. As soon as I connect with someone I'd like to work
with, I'll ask them what's going on in their world. If a conversation
is going well and we connect, we keep going. I never sell them on
what I do. I don't need to.

If there is a way I can support them in that moment, I do—as
powerfully as I would if they had paid me $50,000!—right there

on the spot. I will help them find the answers and dig deep. If the venue is not the appropriate place, I will pull out my calendar and set a time and date when we can continue the conversation.

The coaching starts now. Not when you sign a contract or when you get paid. Coaching is a very intimate profession. It's very delicate and you are working with each other's vulnerabilities. There is no room to half-ass anything. There is no room to wait for a powerful conversation.

Don't put space between you and a potential client because you think they'll see you as an amazing coach once agreements are signed and money has been deposited. Powerful coaching starts NOW. You must WOW them instantly.

I remember my coach telling me that it's not about getting clients, it's about creating a moment where you are never forgotten. With that being said, don't coach anybody if they have not asked for it. That will not make you an awesome coach. That will make you annoying. Keep your coaching powerful and in its place.

When I say "the coaching starts now," I mean create the space where they can feel your presence and strength as a person they will want to see again. It could look a million different ways. It could start by you showing up powerfully and confidently. It could just be you sitting there in silence and listening deeply. It could be letting them know that they are getting in their own way big time, and you may have some ideas to help them remove those blocks. Your job is to create space where they leave saying, "This conversation changed my life!"

When you do that, you won't be short on clients. The coaches waiting for money or waiting to offer the goods later always suffer. I've seen it. If you don't believe me, try it. Have a powerful conversation, follow the rules of Chapters 1 and 2, and see what occurs. It may be your ticket to being the coach you want to be.

I've learned that people will forget what you said, people will forget what you did, but people will never forget how you made them feel.

— Maya Angelou

Chapter 5
Play FULL-OUT

You miss 100% of the shots you don't take.
Wayne Gretzky

This one was a game changer for me. Literally overnight. When I was talking with my coach, I could feel that he had put everything on the line. I could tell that he wasn't going to pull any punches. This was not a coffee shop chat. This was going to be one hour of intense conversation. Our one hour together, as my coach would say, was going to be "high flame." Period.

When you play full-out, you don't have room to be distracted. You don't have time to sit and talk about your problems and how the world is unfair. When you play full-out, everything is fair game and you can't hide behind your weaknesses. Your coach will call you out on them. That's what it means to play full-out.

More on that in a minute.

With every distraction known to man, both outside of our world and inside of our heads, we have every reason and possibility to make up why we can't do what we say we should be doing. This one goes for both coaches and clients. I know so many coaches who do this part-time because they say it's hard to get clients, it's different where they are from, and "it's easy for you to say."

Let's explore the last one for a minute. The idea that "It's easy for you to say." I can't count how many times I get that sentence sent my way. "It's easy for you to say."

Here would be my conversation with potential clients: "It's easy for you to say that all you have to do is start with one simple project and finish it and go to the next. I have kids, a wife, and three dogs to tend to. So, I don't have the luxury of taking it one step at a time."

Or…

"It's easy for you to say that making money is easy. You already have money, and time to do the things you want to do."

Or when it gets personal…

"It's easy for you to say life can be easy and wonderful. You don't have problems like I do and your life is pretty easy."

I used to get offended by all of that. I used to tell my potential clients about all the hardships I went through, and the pain and suffering that got me to where I am now. But the truth is, it never was that painful. Don't get me wrong, I went through what most people would describe as hell; but the truth of the matter is, there is only one way our feelings get processed, which is in our own thinking. The external world has no bearing on how we will FEEL about a particular situation. That's why no two people will feel the exact same way about a bankruptcy, divorce, death, or anything else.

So, as I was going through what most people would say is hell, I didn't become susceptible to the FEELINGS I "should" be feeling with the particular events that were happening. I knew better. In 2007, my brother and I bankrupted our family business. I lost my home, my car, and had to move back to my parents' house. I didn't have a college degree or any credentials, so I didn't know what I could do to move forward. On top of that, I was about 1.8 million dollars in debt to my vendors, family members, and a couple of banks. And yes, they would all call to see when they were going to get their money.

There I was, a supposed entrepreneur and a person who was to coach others to financial success, and I was neither. Was it easy for me to say at the moment that everything was going to be okay? No, it wasn't. But I knew better. I knew that I was not going to be apologetic for where I had gotten myself. I knew that I was going to shake in my bones not knowing what tomorrow was going to look like. But I had one thing that I knew was going to make me or break me. I was going to play 100% full-out and hire mentors and take one step at a time to find the light at the end of the tunnel.

The journey was tough, and knowing my capacity as a man and a driven individual reminded me that it was possible. It became easier and easier as each day showed me new doors and possibilities. I didn't have time to complain to others about my predicament. I didn't have time to blame anyone else in my life. I didn't have time to wallow in my sorrows about what could have been.

I was going to create the story I wanted to live and I did it. I made it "easy for me to say" because that's the story I wanted to end up with. So, each day I made one small change to either save money or make money. I spent time in the business that was falling apart and found one single thing I could change to make the business better. I started to love the employees who worked for me and showed them their value at the worst time of my business. I created loyal customers by sharing my story and asking for help, connections, or assistance. I found people in the same situation I was in who had gotten out, and found out what they did. I made each day a way to succeed.

So, when I hear people say, "It's easy for you to say," it hits me differently. It reminds me of my journey all the way to the point where I am now, where people see me as a success story. The secret throughout my whole journey was that I was already a success story, and I was going to make it a point to succeed even if it was the tiniest step. I was going to make it "easy for me to say" and I was going to prove it to the world!

As a coach, my job is to find out the answer to these questions: Why are you making it so much harder for yourself to say? What's stopping you from playing full-out, no matter the outcome? What does playing full-out mean to you? Can you look yourself straight in the face and say that you are playing full-out?

We hear it all the time about giving it 100%, going when the going gets tough. But when you strip the clichés, what does it really mean? When you play full-out, you don't fear the end result. You don't secretly have dialogues with yourself to justify why you can't ask the client for money. Why can't you move forward to tell someone what you do, and say it proudly?

Playing full-out means that you can put your vulnerabilities in front of you and laugh, or at least look at all of them straight on. Playing full-out means that your clients can see you are transparent in front of them and behind closed doors. Playing full-out does not mean that you act one way in front of your clients, family, and friends and another way when the situation changes. How you appear in the world isn't based on who you are with! Playing full-out means when your client is sitting there telling you about what's going on, you are 100% honest. Sometimes it needs to be brutally honest. When you play full-out and you're present 100%, you'll know exactly what you should say next.

I remember sitting next to a potential client who wanted to let the CEO of her company know that changes needed to happen in her workplace. The company had just merged with another big company and there was a big disconnect with the employees.

I asked her, "What's stopping you?"

She replied that she didn't want to interrupt the CEO and that her voice may not be heard. I paused and told her how uninspiring her story was to me. Here I had a powerful woman who had brought in millions to her company, and she was afraid to have a conversation that may catapult the business to the next level? Before she could continue telling me how powerless she was, I stopped her and made her realize the place she was coming from. It was weak, full of excuses, and I needed to stop her. Why? Because she is more powerful than that.

I was scared out of my mind to have this dialogue. My palms were sweating and my inner voice was telling me to shut up. My heart was beating out of my chest. But I had to tell her. It was my duty. How could I expect her to play full-out if I showed her I couldn't go there first? How could I show her that, despite being afraid and despite feeling overwhelmingly uncomfortable, she should keep going for the greater good?

I was waiting for her to get up and leave the conversation. She didn't. Instead, she absolutely agreed with me that she was showing up from a weak place and she agreed to make a meeting with the CEO and the top leaders and tell them what was on her mind.

I got a call a week later and she was ecstatic. Not only did she spend one hour sharing her views, the top leaders, including the CEO, told her this was needed. The CEO was also feeling disconnected with the employees and didn't know how to bring it up himself. He commended her for stepping up and telling the company leaders what needed to change.

Mahatma Gandhi stated: "Be the change you wish to see in the world." That means that, despite it being uncomfortable, difficult, and emotionally fearful, we go for it anyway. Most of the change we want to see in the world never came easy. Maybe there is something about the hardest things being the most gratifying and life changing.

What else does playing full-out mean? Playing full-out means you're not going into a conversation expecting a client and offering them a false dream in hopes that they will pay your rent or bills. Playing full-out means that you really believe in your coaching to the point that you have your own coach, or have invested in one in the past. (This one has its own chapter.)

Playing full-out means that you can get up from a conversation that is not serving you or your client and move on to one that does. Playing full-out means that you don't go around telling people what you do; you have the courage and strength to SHOW them what you do.

When someone asks me what I do, I may tell them the story of how I raised $30,000 for a nonprofit organization. I may tell them that I can't explain in words what I do, and that if they are open to a two-hour coaching conversation, they will have the chance to experience it. It may be that I connect them with someone who may change their world, whether that's a friend, business partner, or company that might get them closer to their goals. Playing full-out means being ready to sit with someone to whom you promised a powerful coaching conversation, and delivering a powerful session.

I used to be afraid to show them what I do. So, I would resort to my credentials, my awards, and everything I've done in my life. (When you're not playing full-out, it's all about yourself, your ego, and your accomplishments.) Playing full-out means being able to draw the best out of the person in front of you, not telling others about the best in yourself. Playing full-out means that you are willing to step into your fears first before you expect your clients to. Playing full-out means that your ONLY commitment is to serve the person in front of you.

Steve Hardison, a very highly respected coach, states on his website: "Most coaches have a script or a program. These coaches buff, tweak, and improve you or your business—a little. I change lives. I have no set curriculum because you are my material. My program is in your speaking."

I love what he said. "I change lives." When you play full-out, you change lives. That's what your job is as a coach and that's what your job is for yourself.

When I show up for a coaching conversation, I don't come in with preconceived ideas of where the coaching is going to go. I am ready to sit with an open heart and listen; to be bold enough to respond from a place of vulnerability and fear. Usually, I don't take notes. For me personally, if I am taking notes I am not present with my client. So, playing full-out for me also means trusting the moment to give you the answers to take your client to the next level.

Playing full-out also means that when I don't have something to say, I can sit there silently for as long as it takes, until what I need to say shows up. Playing full-out means you are ready to share your deepest secrets, pains, and struggles, and know that your clients can, as well, without having to worry about being judged.

Playing full-out also means creating a space where your client can cry, shout, and spill their deepest desires in a safe place. They should also be aware that you are not going to hold anything back if they do cry, shout, or spill their deepest desires. It will be your job to give them permission to be vulnerable.

If this is too much for you as a coach...I highly suggest you check out other professions. If this is too much for you as a client, then if you were to work with me, I'm 100% sure I wouldn't hire you as a client. I play full-out and so should the people who are investing in coaching.

It's interesting the responses I get when I tell people I am a coach. The initial reaction for many is that it's a laughable profession. It's not. The coaches who have simply decided that all you have to do is call yourself a life coach without playing full-out are what has made this industry laughable to some. Being a coach has a very low entry point, but a very high bar. Unfortunately, the bar is too high for most coaches.

The good news is, when you are a coach who plays full-out and invests in their own coaching, and believes in what they do 100%, your competition is slim. This is important. I eat, sleep, and dream serving my clients. My clients are in my head at all times. The session is just a bonus for my clients.

You will have to have this way of looking at it if you want to be a coach—someone who changes people's lives. And this form of thinking only works in the sphere of playing full-out.

That's it.

PLAY FULL-OUT.

Chapter 6
Go There First

Always bear in mind that your own resolution to succeed is more important than any other.
Abraham Lincoln

I can't count how many times I have met with coaches who want to "coach" others but don't take the time and energy to step into the change they want to see in others. Coaching is not what most think it is. Coaching is a way of life. When my coach talks with me, I know he lives and breathes it. When I talk to my clients, they can see that I live and breathe what I am suggesting to them.

I don't give advice. I give them my clarity from the experiences I've created. Advice is cute. Stepping into the world 100% vulnerable and showing them the side they are afraid to bring out of the shadows is impossible if you can't go there first. That doesn't mean you need to have their problems, issues, or dilemmas. This means that you are ready to give them the arsenal; the dose of what it takes to get out of it—to get someone out of the rut, which is usually a self-illusion they have created. You won't know how to deal with the self-illusion they have created if you haven't taken care of your own self-illusions.

If you are reading this and saying, "Oh, I get it, I'll get to me later,"...you are making a grave mistake. You NEED to jump into the fire. You need to be high flame in your own relationships, your own wealth and health.

I am the best coach you can hire. Why? Because my partner will tell you that I am the best husband she could ever have. Because my family will tell you that I am the best son/brother they could have. Because my staff, my clients, and my business partners will tell you that I am the best associate they could work for. Because when something arises, I challenge it; I handle it like the leader I want my clients to be. Period. I am not afraid to say this to anyone. Are you?

I know this may seem harsh. And it should. You are claiming to change someone else's life. You are in a communion for a common goal. You can't have one if you aren't willing to pay for your share of the ride. It's impossible. I want you to wake up and see your challenges and stand proud to know that you can handle them. I want you to stop having money issues so you can tell your clients the blood, sweat, and tears it took to be financially free. I want you to stop using your old beliefs to justify why you can't be the best coach, so you can proudly, with 100% conviction, tell your clients to stop using their old beliefs.

I recently sat with a coach and asked if he would hire himself for coaching. The answer was NO. That's a problem. Why? Because your clients will see it, your clients will feel it, and so will you. Your results will speak for themselves. This doesn't mean you won't have problems in life. I have just as many problems as my clients. The importance is in the handling.

How do you handle your problems? If your clients were flies on the wall, would they be in awe? Would they learn just by watching you day by day? Would they be proud to call you a coach? Would they want the world to see a day in the life of you?

If it's a NO...fix it! Be the coach you want to coach. Be the coach you want to hire. Today. Right now. This minute.

Go there first. Your world will change and your clients will know you're real.

Chapter 7
Coaching Kings And Queens

I don't know the key to success, but the key to failure is trying to please everybody.
Bill Cosby

When I first became a coach, I thought my job was to help people with their problems. I would help with their relationship problems, work problems, and well-being problems. I was to listen to their problem and help them get out of it. Wow, that was such a problem...

I would listen to my clients' problems and charge them by the hour. Sometimes they would show up, sometimes they wouldn't. Sometimes they would call me to cancel, sometimes they wouldn't.

I had a client I helped with his business problems. I didn't really screen him beforehand. I figured if they were willing to pay for my services (which was $150 per session at that time), then any client was as good as the next. I was so wrong. Any client is not as good as the next. My constant struggle to get the fees I needed proved that. The constant cancellations, excuses, and reasons why change was impossible showed me this.

It's no wonder that coaching for many seems like an uphill battle. I had asked Rich, who at the time was not my coach, how he dealt with clients like that. He said he didn't have clients like that. I was confused. Surely, everyone must have clients like that.

There was one sentence he said to me that changed my whole world, my whole coaching business, and how I showed up in the world. It's that powerful. It was so powerful that before the day was over, I had already ripped up my old business cards. I took down my old website, removed the wording, and changed the name. Everything I had on my website was based on fear. Everything on my old website was based on clients being in a weak place, and I would be their savior and get them out of it.

I started out as a hypnotherapist who claimed that where a person was in their life was not their fault. So, I would get clients who came in with goals like wanting to quit smoking, lose weight, or to stop themselves from biting their nails. To be clear, there is nothing wrong with any of that. The problem wasn't the problem. The problem was the type of clients I was attracting.

Everything on my site put the blame on something outside of themselves. Everything on my site put the guarantee that they would change on me, and that I was willing to pay them their money back if it didn't work. I created a space where I was responsible for their success. So, it was no wonder they would ask for their money back, not show up for appointments, or didn't show up from a place of power when they entered my office.

I couldn't wait to ask Rich how he handled those types of clients. And his response changed everything. That one sentence changed everything. As soon as this insight clicked, I envisioned several clients I would love to coach. Clients who were ready to change. Clients who didn't value our session based on my price, but rather in their investment in themselves. Clients who inspired me in so many ways and excelled in their personal and business lives already.

These were the people I thought were "above" coaching, as if their wealth, their talents, and skills (which are in the top 5% of their specialties or professions) would be against my coaching. I thought that people who were successful wouldn't need my services. After all, they were already successful. What I realized is that the most successful people in the world are the ones who would be the first in line to go to the next level. I realized that the most successful people in the world are the ones who already have mentors and coaches who got them to the place they are now.

I went straight to the people who were the movers in the world, the people who change reality the minute they get an insight. How did I find these people? From this one sentence Rich uttered on stage.

"I only coach Kings and Queens."

Here I was, coaching many who saw themselves as victims, and I couldn't for the life of me figure out why I wasn't connecting with them on any level.

"I only coach Kings and Queens," he said.

That means no more victims, no more playing around with people's problems (although that may suit others), and no more waiting to get paid. I changed my fees to three, six, and 12-month programs and the entry fee to work with me became very demanding. It won't just cost money, it will cost your time, your energy, and your devotion, 100%.

I was showing up to seek Kings and Queens. No more victims. Guess what? They started showing up in my world. I started getting clients who were happy to pay me, happy to work with me for an extended period of time, and excited to move their world to places they never thought possible.

Why?

Because they saw value in changing themselves. So, I would go to the Chamber of Commerce and talk to the president to see what they were struggling with. I would go to nonprofit organizations and find out their biggest fears, and ask them if they would like some support in removing them. I would show up at a business and start a discussion with the owner just to get to know them. When I would go to my doctor's appointment, I would have a conversation with my doctor and offer to give him a book, mp3, or article that I thought might better his business. I would always tell them that if they got an insight, to call me and let me know.

I would be at Starbucks and approach people who were reading a book that inspired me and start a conversation. I would ask my friends and mentors who in their lives inspired them, and then I'd find ways to connect with that person. I would look for people in the world who made me nervous, made me feel excited, or who inspired me in any way. I started coaching Kings and Queens. It was that simple.

So, what is a King or a Queen? Great question.

When I originally sought out clients, I was looking for anyone who responded to my ads, or was willing to pay me. Kings and Queens are different. They don't respond to ads; they seek out extraordinary people. Kings and Queens are already driven, smart, and powerful people. Kings and Queens don't want someone to help them with their smoking problem, they want to expand their world; they want to transform their lives and others.

Kings and Queens aren't looking for advice. They want someone who is brutally honest because they can handle it. Kings and Queens only need one insight and they are off and running, creating a fantastic future. They don't need you to hold their hand.

Kings and Queens might make more money than you, or might have a business that only a small group in our society can handle. Kings and Queens are the movers and shakers of our world. Kings and Queens make me feel nervous, excited, and passionate to be on the coaching journey with them. Kings and Queens DON'T NEED YOU! Kings and Queens know the value of a powerful coach and utilize it.

Who are some people who are Kings and Queens that have utilized a coach?

- Bob Nardelli, CEO of Home Depot
- John Russell, Managing Director of Harley-Davidson in Europe
- Jerome Abarbanel, VP of Executive Resources, Citibank
- Eric Schmidt, CEO of Google
- Most of the top Fortune 500 companies
- Every top athlete and actor
- Every top director and musician

Those are the Kings and Queens. Who else is a King or a Queen?

- Amazing mothers and fathers who value family
- Military men and women who have served our country
- Your neighbor, who wakes up every morning and makes coffee for his wife every day, and opens her door when she gets in the car
- The person sitting across from you at Starbucks who mesmerizes you by their conversation
- The person or organization that makes an impact in our world and leaves it a better place
- The person who simply shares a story and something they said that moved you. That is all that may be needed...
- The person that changed your life

Those are the people I work with. Those are the people who inspire me. There are no exceptions.

There will be some who will say that I am being arrogant. That's okay. I am sharing my story of who I want in my life and the story I want to create. The day I started finding Kings and Queens in my life and offered them an exploration to go deeper, doors opened up that were not possible before. They already believed in themselves and they were willing to seek others who could bring out their gifts.

Find Kings and Queens. Find people who are ready to create something bigger than they could possibly dream of. Help them find the bigger picture; the goal behind the goal. Find Kings and Queens.

This one sentence changed my life, and rocked my world and my coaching practice. If you want to be an extraordinary coach, you need to find extraordinary clients. Show up ready to coach Kings and Queens. Find people who inspire you, move you, and give you chills when you're in the room with them. That's a King or a Queen. You need to be ready to step in with them and move them.

This type of coaching is not for everyone. And my clients are not just anybody. I realized this when I found the Kings and Queens in my life. Make sure that you are a King or a Queen first. Then seek Kings and Queens. Find them, and your world will change.

The job of an educator is to teach students to see vitality in themselves.
— Joseph Campbell

Chapter 8
Tell A Powerful Story

If stories come to you, care for them. And learn to give them away where they are needed. Sometimes a person needs a story more than food to stay alive.
Barry Lopez, in *Crow and Weasel*

My client couldn't get clarity as I was telling him what I thought he should do about his situation with his ex-wife. I know when you are in the midst of an argument that it's hard to see clearly; to make decisions that would serve and honor both the person you are in front of and yourself.

In the midst of our conversation, I told him a simple story that had happened to myself and my girlfriend at the time. We had just gotten a French bulldog. He is the sweetest thing in the world. He would follow us around the house, but he wouldn't dare venture upstairs. Something about the stairs, our Frenchie just hated. He would look at the stairs and watch us go up them. He would growl to let us know that he was upset. We tried putting treats on the stairs, we put him halfway up the stairs and he would freeze. I guess his time would come.

One day, my girlfriend and I were having a heated argument. We got suckered into our thinking and neither of us could get out of it. Every word she would say was making it worse. I wasn't helping the situation, either. As we were talking (more like screaming), I paused for a moment because I felt another body in the room. I looked down and our little baby puppy had slowly made his way up the stairs to see why his mommy and daddy were shouting. He didn't like it.

I don't know what had happened in the moment, but I couldn't get back to the fight. I didn't even remember what we were fighting about. It took the love of our little puppy and his determination to let us know that no fight is worth removing the love we have for each other to get us to pause and change our thinking. In just one instant, the thought we were in about the fight dissolved, just by stopping that thinking in the moment. It just happened to be that our dog showed us how easy it is. We both realized that we were just one thought away from feeling good again. We couldn't get back into the argument because a new thought had already taken the place of the old one.

I realized then that we are always just one thought away from feeling anything. And the only way to stop yourself from getting a new thought is sticking with the old one and trying to fix it. I told this to my client and he started to weep. I couldn't have told him any other way. How trivial any argument is in the moment, however meaningful they may seem initially. I couldn't have given him an exercise or a chart that would have shared this universal love that even puppies know about. I just shared a story and let him be a part of it.

We all have a powerful story, and it may be so powerful that you can change someone's view, their life, and their world. Share your stories. There are hidden gifts in each one. Make them powerful. Go deep into the story. Share what you went through; how it affected you. Share the pain. Be vulnerable. Talk about it like you are living it again. Get goose bumps. This is what Coach Steve Chandler says is the distinction between information vs. transformation. It's moving them to a place called "possible" without them even knowing it.

You have stories that can change the person sitting in front of you. You want them to move to a place? Show them it's possible with a story. My coach spends so much time cultivating my stories. He knows the power in them. He knows the hidden gems that others will get from them. Sometimes my own stories make me a better person, just by retelling them.

Once your clients get a glimpse of your powerful story, it's your turn to cultivate theirs. Bring it back to life and show them what a story can do for them. Create a new story for them in real time. Let them mold their stories from the past and connect them with the present. If you don't know how to bring a story out of your client, ask them, "What don't you want me to know about you?" Then dive deep.

I'll go first. What I don't want you to know about me is that six months before I proposed to my wife, I found out that I was taking a drug that completely crashed my endocrine system. I was taking a drug called Finasteride for male pattern baldness, and the side-effects (I later found out) were low libido, low energy, and even the possibility of never being able to have kids.

I later was diagnosed with Post Finasteride Syndrome (PFS). It's devastating for people who have experienced it, and unfortunately it's so bad that some people who have it commit suicide. All this so I could save the hair on my head. I was so pissed off! Here I was, a 34-year-old man, and I had the sex drive and ambition of an 80-year-old.

Imagine just getting engaged, and you can't have an erection at all. Instead, you sit there and wonder how you got yourself to this place, and how stupid it was to not research the drugs you were putting into your mouth. Imagine having thoughts of having children, then holding that thought until the test results come in so that you know you have enough sperm to create a child.

Imagine all of your friends telling you stories of their sexual encounters and their excitement with their partners, and here you are, taking drugs just to get your hormones back to normal, whatever that means.

I was devastated. I stopped coaching for a bit because I couldn't get myself out of the rut. That was until I realized that so many others are going through what I was going through, and it's my duty to help others. I called my doctor and told him that I was willing to share my pain with his other patients if he was open to it. He was ecstatic. Most of his patients are embarrassed, shy, and secretive about their condition. After all, who wants to talk about not being turned on by women and not being able to have erections anymore?

I would get on the calls and just share with them. I didn't want to have a pity party and the men on the other line could hear that I didn't consider myself a victim. We would talk about things I never would have thought to talk about previously. Things like whether he masturbated, how flaccid his penis was, and the consistency of his sperm. These were not things I ever thought I'd discuss with a stranger.

The worst part of it was that I knew exactly what they were going through. But I showed them that vulnerability has power. I showed them that not being embarrassed about what they were going through showed them how powerful they really are. I shared with them that as soon as I found out what had happened to me, I found a way to empower myself by empowering others. Many of the people who would have never been open about what had happened to them called me back to tell me that they were now helping others.

I was terrified to tell others about what I was going through, but I did it anyway. I was embarrassed to be going through sexual dysfunction at my age, but I realized by being transparent and real, the pain transformed to empowerment.

What I don't want you to know about me is that I deleted this whole chapter a few times because I wasn't sure if I wanted the world to know this about me.

What I don't want you to know about me is that I am going to tell my PFS story anyway, because my vulnerability in sharing this story is worth it if it enables me to share my most vulnerable moments with people who need to hear it.

Since sharing my story, men from all walks of life have opened up and told me their sexual problems. Many who kept it a secret are now getting help. What a shame to keep in your most vulnerable stories. What a shame that the most valuable thing that moves someone else to action is something we keep inside of us out of fear.

What if the people who were going through what I am going through didn't fall victim to their insecurities and showed up and told others about what was going on with them? What if one of them had talked to me before I had taken the drug?

I told several of my friends who were taking the drug about my side-effects. ALL of them told me they were going through the same thing. Why the hell didn't they tell me? Because they said they felt insecure. What a shame. What a devastating shame. Some of our insecurities are literally killing people!

I can't stand for that. I am sharing with the world. Why? Because sharing is transformative. In my case, life saving.

Alan Watts said, "For God's sake, tell us something that will save us from ourselves. Take a deep breath and tell us your deepest, darkest secret, so we can wipe our brow and know that we're not alone."

When you allow your clients to become vulnerable and you give them a container in which to feel safe, they are not alone. You have stories that are the same. And unless you can go there with your clients, don't expect them to go there first. Share your strongest, most terrifying stories and go deep with them. Feel the pain of your stories and go deeper. Let it stir your stomach; let your thoughts in your head tell you to shut up...and continue

36

anyway.

I am my stories, and a powerful story is the fuel that moves me. Help your clients see their powerful stories. Move them to a story they have never imagined living. You can do that. Stories are limitless. Stories shed our vulnerabilities and show us a side of ourselves we've never seen. Stories can connect us, mold us, and save lives. They are the creators of the soul.

Chapter 9
Dreaming A Bigger Dream

Without leaps of imagination, or dreaming, we lose the excitement of possibilities. Dreaming, after all, is a form of planning.
Gloria Steinem

When I set up my initial meeting, I want to know about my potential client's dreams. I want to know about the dream behind the dream. I've heard of many coaches who want to tackle their clients' problems. Why? Why would you want to work with people's problems?

Work on their dreams, and their problems will go away as a side-effect of dreaming. Why is that? Our dreams get us connected to a future. They allow us to find resources from a place that isn't tarnished. Our dreams have no rules. We don't have to worry about getting judged, hurt, or being afraid. After all, they're just our dreams...

But our dreams are not just dreams. They are a gateway to our reality. Our dreams allow us the possibility of what is, right now.

Most of us spend too much time in the problems of our lives. We are struggling, fixing, and thinking. Our creativity gets blocked. Nothing pours out. Our dreams remove our blocks and take us back to what can be. No struggling, fixing, or thinking.

Look at someone who is daydreaming. They are peaceful, relaxed, and out of this world. Their creative side is kicking in. Our insights live there. So, become a dream-maker for your clients. Put their dreams so close to them that they can feel it. Don't stop their dream once they have told you about it. Go deeper and color their dream. What does the dream mean to them in five years, 10 years, or for the rest of their life? What does the dream mean to them NOW? How can you get them closer to their dream?

As Rich Litvin once told me, "Find out their biggest dream and have them make the smallest step toward their dream right now."

I remember when I was afraid of public speaking. I was so afraid that on my way to one of my first speaking engagements, I hoped I'd get into a car crash. I would rather be in a hospital than in front of people speaking. At least I could endure the pain of broken bones. That's until I figured out my dream for myself. Find the dream that's bigger than your clients' problems, fears, hurts, and pains, and you'll have a client for life. After my first speaking engagement, while driving home, I asked myself why I wanted to speak. What was my dream?

I wanted to share my story, my successes, and my failures. I didn't want to be the most polished speaker. I wanted to move people. I wanted to serve people. I wanted to change people's lives. I could feel my body change. Was I still scared? Of course I was. But you can't come between me and my dreams. I won't let you. But...I needed a dream bigger than me to find this out.

Your dreams will give you courage, fuel, and strength. They will also make you playful and alive. Look at kids. They love magic, dreams, and fairytales. It's part of our innocence and our hearts at play. We forget the power of our dreams. We forget that our dreams allow us to prove the world wrong. They stop us from following the status quo.

Do you remember what Martin Luther King said in his famous speech? "I have a dream!" He didn't say, "I have a plan" or "I have some suggestions." It was a *dream* that he shared.

Find your clients' dreams. When you discover your clients'

dreams...they won't let their fears, hurts, and pains get between them and their dreams, either.

Sydney Banks, a theosophist and founder of *The 3 Principles,* so eloquently stated that his job was to gently "tap people on the shoulder and wake them from the dead." He would wake them up and have them dreaming. We don't only dream when we are asleep. Dreams are more powerful when we are awake—when we can move, dance, and speak with our dreams. Find your clients' BIGGEST dreams. Then go deeper and find the dream behind the dream. Dreams are the soul behind our lives. Then allow your clients to find the action behind the dream. The bigger the dream, the faster you want them to act. Make the dream BIG! Give them one action to get them closer to their dream.

I recently had a client who wanted to change the atmosphere of her workplace. She was high up the corporate ladder, but she didn't like what she was seeing. The communication with her employees was severely strained because people were knee-deep into paperwork and getting the next deal. Her boss was disillusioned because his co-workers were afraid to approach him for fear that they may lose their jobs. She went from being the top seller in her business to wanting to quit her job. I knew what I needed to do. I let the water in her mind settle and after a minute of silence I asked her what she wanted. What was her dream?

She said she wanted to have the best job in the world. She wanted to walk in and know that everyone was onboard and excited to work on the next project. She wanted the CEO to know what was happening at work and for him to assist in making her place of work amazing. So, I asked her, "What's the first step closer to having an amazing workplace?"

She sat for a minute, then said, "I need to get the CEO, my employees, and all the key people in one room and let them know what I want. And I am going to be damn sure that our workplace is going to be amazing."

I asked her what her action plan would be to make this happen. The next day she went to the CEO and said that she needed him and all the key people in a room for at least one hour. She was trembling as she said this, because nobody went to the CEO with such a request; especially during their busy time. To her surprise, the CEO was ecstatic and looked forward to the meeting. He congratulated her for showing up with conviction and for wanting to make a change.

She had a dream, and my job was to create the first part of the action. I needed her to see that this one action would get her closer to her dream. Dreams start with the first action plan. But you have to know your clients' dreams.

Your coaching conversation for the rest of the session is the action plan. That will be enough. Getting someone closer to their bigger dream is enough. Taking them closer to the next step toward their dream is enough. It will help them remove their fears, insecurities, and doubts because these will become less relevant. How nice to be able to work on someone's dreams instead of their problems.

I don't work on my client's problems. I work on their dreams. Find out your own dream and find out who your dream client is, and get them! How? Just ask your client, "What's your biggest dream, if nothing mattered, such as money, family, job security, etc.?"

Sit silently and let them unfold their dream. Then help them get there. Become a part of the Dream Team.

If you have built castles in the air, your work need not be lost; that is where they should be. Now put the foundations under them.
— Henry David Thoreau

Chapter 10
If It's Not A Right Fit...

I mean, if the relationship can't survive the long term, why on earth would it be worth my time and energy for the short term?
Nicholas Sparks

I remember when I first started coaching. I thought I could change the world and everyone in it. I would go around telling people what I did and ask them to give me their toughest problems. I cringe even writing about it! I remember my intuition telling me that the potential client who wanted to work with me should not be my client.

I didn't listen to my own advice. I figured that where there is a will, there is a way. It may be the case, but I am here to have a dream life. And if my client isn't a part of my dream life, then I will find someone else. If what they want from the coaching sessions isn't on par with what you want, it's time to tell them that it may not be a right fit.

In this profession, there's sometimes an assumption that the more people you've coached, the better coach you are. That's nonsense. If you have the ability and capacity to have one powerful client and rock their world, I'd trade that for 100 mediocre clients with little or minimal life changes. Don't work to get your number higher. Work on getting the client who fits in with your life—the one that makes you move to a better place; the person who inspires you and connects with you on different levels.

This is not a race to get as many clients as you can. This is a serious profession to change someone's life. If you become selective in your coaching and find the person who moves you and with whom you connect, you won't be short on clients.

Why?

Because they will tell everyone about you. They will be your ally. They will know the type of clients you coach, your rules and your selectiveness with your clientele. If you are just anybody's coach, you are going to get just anybody wanting advice.

I don't give advice. I change lives. In order to change lives, you need to be very selective. My coach only works with five devoted clients a year. Only five!

Why?

Because he knows they will move to great heights. He can tell that the five clients he coaches are extraordinary men and women. He doesn't need any more than the five.

I was honored to be one of the five. That's how your clients should feel. They should be honored to work with you. Coaching takes dedication, work, and action. It's an honor for both parties. Don't lose sight of that. If you think this is just a numbers game, you're in the wrong game.

Sure, I know coaches who have tons of clients. There is nothing wrong with that. But...I don't want you to believe that you *need* to have hundreds of clients. Having a handful of powerful clients may be enough for you to be the powerful coach you want to be.

I love what Steve Hardison wrote on his website: "How many clients do I have? One. The one I'm with."

It's not a numbers game. It's what you can do with the one you have in front of you. This changed my world. It also allowed me to let potential clients know that they may not be a right fit.

It's okay if something with the potential client doesn't resonate with you. Sometimes that's what a potential client needs to hear. It may be that they will be a better fit in the future, but don't make them your client until it's a right fit. You'll know when it is. Listen to your instincts.

When I first became a coach, I was so busy trying to fill up my client list that I rushed some of my client connections. I was already thinking about my next client. Never again. I am now confident that I can live having only one client. I will be so selective with who works with me, that this one client will change his or her life and remember me for the rest of theirs. I will be so selective with my clients that I have no choice but to have a success story. When you do that, you won't be short on clients.

Try it! Try this paradoxical idea. Be so selective with your clientele that you won't be short on clients.

Chapter 11
Build A Relationship, Not A Client

The meeting of two personalities is like the contact of two chemical substances: if there is any reaction, both are transformed.
Carl Jung

Nobody likes to be sold to, and yet people can't get this one out of their heads. It's so cliché to build a relationship, but nobody seems to get this one right. *Maybe if I pretend to build a relationship and secretly sell them my products, goods, or services...I'll make money.* That's not how it works. Wow people so much that they will want to work with you.

I recently signed up a new client. Before I signed him up, I had already sent him a book that changed my world. It's actually written by my coach Rich Litvin, called *The Prosperous Coach*. He wrote me back and told me that he'd already booked clients. He was making money before he'd even worked with me.

Why is that important? Because I was now a part of his transformation even *before* we started our work together. His life shifted and I was involved.

Send your clients a book that will shift their world. Send them a YouTube clip that will change their lives at work. Offer them an mp3 of something that you know will excite them.

GIVE, GIVE, GIVE!

Then invite them to a conversation about what you sent them and take it deeper. Find the connection to what you have sent them and the future they want to create. Do this before you've signed them up. Then offer them something else!

I have dozens of books in my car that have changed my life. About three times a week I take one of these and give it to someone. I have gotten more clients out of just giving them a book, and them sharing what they got out of it, than any Internet funnel or cheap marketing trick.

Why?

Because I really care about what I am offering and the book I give them has to have meaning to me. It needs to be a real effort to want to move the people you connect with. No marketing. Just wowing them.

Wow them on the spot. Wow them so much that they will want to find out what else would make their life amazing. Maybe as part of their wonderful life they will buy your product, services, or your coaching. Even if they decide not to work with you at the moment, you were still a part of their transformation. You will not be forgotten. That's how you build a relationship.

I've had people come to me for my coaching services a year after we initially met. I was still on their mind. I've also had clients refer me and rave about me to the point where the person they were speaking to wanted to connect with me.

One of my favorite coaches, Steve Chandler, once told me, "Leave every conversation with an impact and you will never be short on clients."

Impact them by shifting their lives with a gift, a book, an audio, a song, or a powerful coaching conversation that will blow their minds—whatever you see fit for the person in front of you that will take them to a place they never thought possible.

When you genuinely have the interest of the person in front of you as the sole motivator, there is no such thing as a "client." Not in coaching. You should not have a client in that sense. What I mean is, you should be such a power source in their lives that they have no other option but to want to move forward with you.

This is faster than any elevator pitch. This is more powerful than any sales tactic. Why? Because it's neither. It's only about you and the person in front of you. There is no room to sell them anything. If you are selling them you are not serving them. That means I don't have a "free" consultation; I offer them a powerful coaching session. That means I don't have a discount on my services; I will have a powerful conversation to move them to create the money on their own accord. That means that after our coaching term is complete, I sit with them and see if there is another dream they want to create. If not, we part ways until further notice.

I will continue to serve them. That's it. The whole world is an opportunity to serve. Let others do the selling. You won't.

My coach once read a quote that stated, "Don't do what everyone else is doing; be the only one that does what you do."

If you serve your clients with your most powerful gifts, you won't have competition. The price will become irrelevant. If you are selling, now you are in competition; your prices can be compared, the hours can be compared, the value can be compared. Compared to what? The other guy who is selling his services.

Don't sell your coaching unless you want to spend the whole time telling them the value of your coaching. While you're wasting your time in that conversation, I am already making their dreams a reality. Don't get stuck in that conversation. Move it back to serving them. Move it back to their dreams. Make it possible for them and be a part of their journey. You won't need to sell them anything. They'll be onboard before you can even tell them about your coaching services.

I never cease to be amazed at the power of the coaching process to draw out the skills or talent that was previously hidden within an individual, and which invariably finds a way to solve a problem previously thought unsolvable.
— John Russell,
Managing Director, Harley-Davidson Europe Ltd.

Chapter 12
Get A Coach

It's comical how many coaches I know that tell me life coaching is so important for relationships, wealth, and health; and when I ask them who their life coach is, they tell me they've never had one. Who are you to tell me coaching is valuable when you yourself don't believe in it?

This could be the most important chapter you read. Get a coach! Your life will not be the same. Your coaching will never be the same. When you get a coach, you will enter a level of understanding that was previously not available to you. I would never hire a coach who doesn't have a coach or hasn't had a coach.

You need to believe in your own product. I have had several coaches. I have made huge monetary investments in my coaches. Why? Because I believe in the power of coaching. My wealth coach made me more money. I was in bankruptcy. I had to sell my car, my house, and put my head down to figure out what I had done wrong.

At a time when you don't have money, how does it make sense to give money to someone? Because having a coach is the fastest way to get you where you want to go. "One step at a time," my coach told me. What do we need to do today to get me back to being prosperous? The first step—just for today?

He would give me a list and had me do it. First we sold my car—a brand new convertible Mercedes—and got something economical. I sold my house and got rid of my mortgage. I had to close down three of my restaurants. That was so hard for me. We put so much effort into having those restaurants that I didn't want to see them close. My employees were crying. I was crying. But my coach didn't falter. He wasn't there to invest in my emotional affairs, but to fix the bleeding. He was there to straighten out what I had created.

The list went on and on and I couldn't have done it without my coach. I couldn't have done it because I was blinded by my emotional vision; what I thought I should be doing. He removed the "shoulds" in my life and went back to needs. What *needed* to be done to be prosperous. One step at a time. I couldn't have done it without a coach.

My life coach made me a better man and reminded me of how I should show up in the world. With each phone call and each conversation, my life coach would cut through my stories and allow me to see that I didn't need to buy into all my stories. Stories of how coaching is difficult; how I don't have enough experience to go into a corporation and talk to them about fundraising. I'd never done a fundraiser, but I showed them how to connect with their donors. My coach showed me it's about connections. He showed me my value and didn't let me get bogged down with my bullshit.

It got to the point that I felt like he was with me, even when we hadn't spoken for weeks. I actually told him that during one of our phone conversations.

He responded and told me, "It's not that I am with you and that's why you're more powerful; it's that you've given yourself permission to be the powerful person you've always been, but didn't see."

My coach created a space where I could be vulnerable without judgment. He created a container where it was safe to tell him things I had never shared with anyone else. My coach created a container where everything is fair game. Sharing my wildest dreams, scariest issues, and deepest vulnerabilities with a person who is 100% there just for you is transformative. My life coach gave me permission to grow in places that I wasn't giving myself access to. He made it clear that fear is normal, but doesn't have to get in the way of creating a wonderful life.

My marketing coach showed me how marketing really works without marketing (how ironic). He would sit me in his office for hours, sometimes a whole day, and show me how I could serve my clients. If I strayed from the conversation, he would get me back on track. I was able to change the whole dynamic of my brick-and-mortar business because of my coach.

I got coaches. I hired them. I paid for them and I made action plans to succeed. My coaches would sit with me and ask me what I really wanted. They would press deeper to see if what I said was what I really wanted. My coaches would listen to me spit out nonsense about why I couldn't do what I wanted, and smile. They would let me see the silliness of my arbitrary limitations.

My coaches made a problem a project. Sometimes our problems seem never-ending because we are in them. My coaches made it fun, energizing, and easy to finish because I had someone who believed in me even when I didn't believe in myself.

I know what it takes for my clients to succeed because I hired coaches. I know what it's like to have someone watching over you, making sure you don't mess yourself up. I know what it takes to finish a task that you committed to with someone else. I know what it takes to sit with a client and tell them that their stories are bullshit and that I'm not buying them, because my coaches had to tell me that same thing. And I am so glad they did when others didn't.

Why?

Because they wanted me to succeed and now I know what it takes for me to help others succeed. I've been on both sides of the fence. You also need to do it.

I have a friend who "coaches" but doesn't want to invest in a coach. He keeps telling me he should and he wonders why he is having trouble getting clients. I told him there is something behind your words when you don't believe in your own product. People can hear above the words. They can tell you don't have a coach. They can taste it. He wants people's money but doesn't want to invest in it himself. He tells others that coaching will make them successful, but doesn't believe coaching will make him successful. What a shame.

Get a coach, right now! How do you find a coach? Find someone who lives the way you dream to live. The one who lives their coaching and shows up in the world in a way that moves you. You're coaching will never be the same after that. You will truly see what it means to be a coach. You will see what it means to truly change a life.

Get a coach to change your life first. Dive in head-on and see what it means to be a client; see what it means to be able to move beyond your own possibilities and limitations. This is the best way to become a better coach. If you listen to only one piece of advice in this book, this is the advice I would have you follow.

Chapter 13
There Are No Rules

Hell, there are no rules here—we're trying to accomplish something.
Thomas A. Edison

Wat are the rules if a potential client doesn't call you back? What are the rules if your initial session with a potential client didn't go well? What are the rules if your client was ready to pay and invest in coaching, but they decided to not return your calls or emails? What are the rules if you are stuck, you don't have the answer, or you're not sure what to say to the person sitting in front of you?

What are the rules?

Go to the bookstore and you'll find a list of coaching books that tell you what you should say, the proper body posture for confidence, and a host of other tools needed to have a successful practice. Want to know the secret? There are no rules. There is no one correct way to handle the same problem the same way every time.

If there are no rules, how should we handle anything? What about all the scenarios I mentioned above? Surely, there is something that could make those scenarios better.

Yes, there is. It's knowing that you have the answers within you at that moment, to step into the fear, and talk to the person in front of you, being 100% transparent.

You might say, "Wait, Amir...didn't you say there are no rules? Isn't that a rule that you just made?"

I did.

When there are no rules, you can also break them. It's

paradoxical, I admit. Get used to it. And let your client get used to knowing that there are no right answers, and to stop waiting for them. If you start from a place of 100% transparency, 100% commitment to serve the person in front of you, 100% from love and compassion, and 100% of not giving a shit (besides giving your best to uphold all of the above), then the right answer will show up in that moment.

People want a prescription for what to do in those moments of uncertainty. Your job is to show up as the person who can resolve anything. Period. It's not a prescription of what to do, it's a *DESCRIPTION* of where you are coming from. When your conviction is to serve—I mean serve the hell out of the person in front of you—the answers will show up.

I recently had a coaching call with a potential client. He was 100% all-in for coaching. He'd already committed to pay. I sent him my payment information. Nothing came through. I waited for a few more days. Nothing.

Of course, when this happens you want to listen to the chatter in your head; the one that tells you that you didn't do a good enough job, you're asking for too much money, or maybe they didn't really care about coaching.

All sorts of stuff goes through a coach's head.

So, what did I do? I broke my own rule and stopped listening to the voices. I sent out a short email. "Can you call me today at 10:00 a.m.? 760-555-5555."

That's it.

I knew that I wouldn't be able to be 100% transparent over the email. I also knew that my potential client deserved more than an email.

The phone rang. I picked up. I simply asked him, "How can I serve you today?"...and waited.

He wasn't sure what I meant, so I told him.

"I may have not served you enough. I sense you are having doubts about coaching. How can I best serve you today?"

I was correct. He was having doubts. And we spent the rest of the phone call talking about all the doubts and fears and expectations.

I was so proud of him for showing up the way he did. He was afraid of telling me. As a coach, I want him to be afraid, and say it anyway. The conversation became powerful. But, I needed to step into the fear first and tackle it firsthand. Without rules. Just connecting. Not waiting for an outcome. Not waiting to "sell" him on my services. Just connecting, however that looked to me, in that moment, jumping into that place with my potential client and knowing that we were both in the same place and that we were both going to come out better.

The conversation was a life changer for him. He went against his own rules and showed up 100% full-out! He let his guard down and shared his fears and doubts. He told me it was the best coaching session he'd ever had.

Why?

Because there are no rules. I wasn't expecting anything. I just wanted to serve him the best I could at that moment.

Do you want to be a better coach? Forget the rules and look your client straight in the eye and step into a place of serving. Step into the place that makes you uncomfortable; a place where you don't hold any punches. Do it from a place of love. There are few people who will go this deep with them. That's why they are sitting with you. That's why they want a coach. Be that person for them. Change the game; play the game. Hell...there are no rules when you and your client become the game.

Chapter 14
Create High-Value Agreements

*You only exist because of the agreements you made with yourself
and with the other humans around you.*
José Luis Ruiz

If you read Chapter 4, then you know that there is no better time to have a coaching mentality than NOW. There is no waiting until after the 5th meeting. There is no waiting until you have disagreements to disrupt a powerful conversation that was not happening because there were no high-value agreements set in place. My clients know exactly what they are getting into. As far as the results, I'm not sure what they are going to look like, but they are always extraordinary.

The reason we get a difficult client stems back to the original agreements that were set in place by both parties. My initial meeting before we dive into coaching is spent setting aside at least two hours going through our agreements. The more agreements that are set in place, the fewer uninvited expectations show up that can dramatically dampen the power of a coaching conversation.

You are not in the business of hashing out problems. You are in the game of changing someone's life. When you hold that much responsibility, you need to take care of the agreements beforehand and make sure there are no loose ends. What types of agreements? How will you be contacting them? Are you connecting via phone, email, Skype, or in person? What will your client expect as you move forward with your coaching? How long will the sessions last and what needs to be done after a session (i.e., an actionable step from the conversation or a specific targeted question regarding the coaching call or session). In what months are you working with them? Are there any breaks in-between for any reason? What is your response time if they have a question, comment, or concern?

I had a coaching client who was frantic and wanted me to pick up the phone whenever he called. That wasn't part of our agreement. I had to remind him that I would respond within a 24-hour time frame, and that there should not be any expectation otherwise. I don't work on expectations. I work only on agreements. He understood.

That particular incident didn't happen again because I stand firm on my agreements. Other aspects of the agreements are the energy and time you expect your client to invest. Do you want them to record the sessions? Do you meet at the same place? If so, why or why not?

I sometimes change my locations because I don't like the stale environment of an office. I'll go to a nearby luxurious hotel or the beach. But we talk about that in our agreements. We make the agreements visible and we make sure we are both on the same page, each and every time I sign up a client.

Chapter 15
Don't Decide Their Breakthroughs

Patience is power.
Patience is not an absence of action;
rather it is "timing"
it waits on the right time to act,
for the right principles
and in the right way.
Fulton J. Sheen

I am a go-getter. I like speed. I like waking up and going for it 100%. My issue was that I assumed everyone worked that way. During my early years as a coach, I would rush people to "get it." Surprisingly, the more information I would feed into a client's head, the less they got it.

It's funny how the system works. The good part about the system is that once you understand it, you can tap into it indefinitely.

I started to slow down and not worry about a breakthrough. It's not about my timing, it's not about my insight, and it's not for me to decide my clients' breakthroughs. As coaches, we want to help—we want to push and bring the best out of our clients. We want to have them see what they never thought possible. But you have to make it a dance. You have to guide the person in front of you with the right steps. It needs to be chaotic and systematic at the same time. If you tell them what their steps need to be 10 steps later, they will get lost. If you tell them that they need to hurry up their dance, it won't look like dancing anymore. If you want to connect on the dance floor, they will have to bring their own uniqueness to the table.

Coaching is the same way.

It's not your job to decide when their breakthroughs should be, how they're going to look, and what the end result should be. That's good news for us. That means our job is to ONLY be present and committed to listening and learning. That's it—learning the inner workings of what the client is trying to say, discovering your client's true desires, discovering and having a childlike curiosity of going deeper with their question, and asking them if they are open to exploring that thought a bit deeper.

I had a client who had a question about a divorce situation. We ended up talking about surfing and the connection between worrying about what wave to ride, and not putting more importance on one wave over another. After all, as soon as one wave passes, another one will come along. Waves are like opportunities; they always show up and your job is to ride them when they come.

Now, I wasn't worried about talking about the divorce at that moment as we talked about surfing. For a moment, I felt insecure because I thought I hadn't coached him properly. I was ready to go back to the divorce, but I'm glad I didn't. I sat with him. I could see he was letting the thoughts in his head settle. He started to see correlations between the surfing metaphor and his divorce. He would smile and make an "agreement" gesture.

I just waited.

After about 10 minutes, he said, "I know what I need to do with my divorce. Thank you, Amir."

I let him decide the meaning of our conversation. I let him sit with this new breakthrough. It would have looked way different to me. But it wasn't my breakthrough and it wasn't my moment. It was my client's time for a breakthrough.

The biggest gift I have gotten from my coach is to give less in the conversation so clients have room for a breakthrough. And if they don't have a breakthrough right that minute...wait. Don't overpower the conversation. Don't try to force your brilliance on them. It won't work. Less is more. Wait for it. Wait and don't decide their breakthroughs.

Sometimes I get caught up and I forget. The excitement kicks in and I want to share everything I know. I want to "prove" to them the type of coach I can be. Those are the moments I feel disconnected. Those are the moments where my potential client has to "think" about working with me. They are actually not thinking at all. They have already made a decision.

Why?

Because I didn't allow them time to decide the value of the conversation. I didn't allow them to plant the seeds of transformation. I over-watered the garden of insights and now all the insights are dead. Now they'll have to "think" their way out of working with me.

I don't blame them. I don't blame the ones I did that with. I recommend you don't do it. You'll need to step back and start over again. Step back, ask them how you can support them; how you can make the conversation amazing again. Put the ball in their court. Put the opportunity for insights and transformations in their space. And most importantly, don't wait for a breakthrough to happen. Just serve them 100%. Just be committed to them full-out. The powerful breakthrough will emerge when it's ready. Your job is to create the environment for growth. Their job is to come up with the insight. Don't decide it for them, and you'll have a client for life.

How to Be Good At Anything:

If you wish to be a writer, write.
— Epictetus

(If you wish to be an extraordinary coach, coach!)

Chapter 16
Get Them In Front Of You

The single biggest problem in communication is the illusion that it has taken place.
George Bernard Shaw

We can be our worst enemies when it comes to getting clients. With having a multitude of ways to communicate with a potential client, we have given away the art of connecting. We can Facebook them, Tweet them, Instagram, Yelp, or text them. There are so many different ways to communicate. But there are only a few ways to *connect*.

We email our clients a lengthy proposal because we think that if they have it in email format, they won't forget it. Wrong. When it goes to their email, it's a great way for them to make a two-second decision whether they want to read it at that moment or toss it aside.

Why?

Because they have 15 other proposals to look at; 28 other to-do lists to figure out, and now you have another one to offer them with your lengthy email telling them what their next steps are, or giving them a beautifully written chapter on how their life is going to be amazing with your coaching.

Don't do it.

I know it sounds tempting. The magic will always happen when they are in front of you. Get them in a position of real-time interaction. Have them make their decision with you around. Have decisions and calendar appointments made on the spot.

Most other coaches put distance between themselves and their clients. They want to be polite. They say things like, "Oh, I can imagine you're busy right now. Why don't I text you the time I can email you, so we can put something on the calendar and have a phone call?"

Don't do it.

Pull out your calendar and make it easy. "I have Tuesday at 9:00 a.m. open. Can you make it? No? Okay, how about Tuesday at 2:00 p.m.? Yes. Okay, great. Please contact me on Tuesday at 2:00 p.m."

It's that easy.

If a potential client tries to put distance between you, make it so you become closer. If they say, "Please email me the dates that work for you," tell them to call you when they have their calendar available.

Be the coach right this minute. Move decisions on your time. Clients like that. Make commitments and let them know that you don't dilly-dally with your time. You create coaching conversations and there is no need to wait for them. Make the appointment now.

I remember Supercoach Michael Neill explaining the importance of getting your clients in front of you. He said, "Coaching is like sex; it's always better in person, although it's okay to have it sometimes via a phone call."

I like that. It's true. Don't create this idea that you are some esoteric coach, imagining abundance will somehow get you there. It won't. The only way to get abundance is to have a client. The only way to have a client is to get them in real time. The only way to move them with a powerful coaching conversation is to have them in front of you.

The best is in person. If that doesn't work, get them on the phone. Email should be used sparingly. Most coaches use email and they wonder why they can't book coaching calls or why they aren't filled in their practice. When you hide behind a computer you are sending a message that you are not powerful enough to show up in their world and be vulnerable. You are afraid to ask for money, so an email will sound more courteous and polite. You are afraid to get them to commit to a time to change their lives. So, you use a weak position so as not to "bother" them.

If your clients are feeling bothered, then you are not showing up powerfully in their lives. If you feel a disconnect with your clients, and you're in a position where all you've done is emailed them...it's not too late. Write them one last time and say, "I have something important to share with you. Call me: 760-555-5555."

Once they call you, let them know that you've not served them the way you could have (because you were hiding behind your emails), and that you'd love to have a conversation about their world and how you can be of support in it. Then, set it up on the calendar, right there on the spot.

Get used to doing this. Make it like clockwork. If someone asks what you do, tell them right then and there that you'd love to show them and that you are available on Wednesday or whatever day. Don't give them "hints" of what you do to sound mysterious. Don't try to be "professional" and soft spoken and see where the conversation leads when it comes to coaching.

Most importantly...

Don't make the mistake of moving the conversation away from them by saying you're going to email them. You will lose their enthusiasm and you'll be competing with all their other emails. Stand out and be **bold.** Make the person in front of you commit. Show up like you mean business. Show up like you have something that will blow their mind. That's your job. You're not selling them an ad in the yellow pages. You are about to move their world in a way they have never known possible.

The coaching starts right at that minute, by taking charge of your time and the potential client's time. Move them to where they want to be *right this minute*. That means don't put a barrier between you when it's not necessary.

That's right.

No I'll email you, Tweet you, Facebook you, or send you a message in a bottle. Don't put a barrier there.

I've had clients thank me for being persistent. Why? Because their inaction is the exact thing they wanted me to help them with in their lives, right this minute. I was their first step in showing them what "powerful immediate action" looks like. I was their first glimpse at not allowing technology or anything else to get in the way of serving them.

It's your job to get them in front of you. That's why they need you. That's why they are going to hire you. This is going to be their first glimpse of what they should expect moving forward with you.

Put it all on the line. Get them to act, get them to move to places they didn't think they could. How will you be able to get them to do that? By getting them in front of you, so you or your clients don't have an excuse for not taking action.

So, go to your email or your phone book right now and close the gap. Tell them you have something important to share with them or simply connect with them and ask them about their world. Have a real-time conversation with them right now.

It's that easy.

Have a powerful real-time conversation *right now.*

Chapter 17
Be Bold

Fortune favours the bold.
Virgil

O ne of my close friends and mentors, Reggie Lal, is a prominent real estate investor. When I was going through a 1.8 million dollar debt, his coaching and wisdom guided me through a time in my life where I knew I wouldn't be able to do it without another set of eyes. One of the things he taught me was to be bold. Ask questions and seek advice regardless of what you think of yourself or what others will think about you.

I remember a story he told me about when he was first getting into real estate investing. He would seek out specific real estate specialists—specialists everyone would love to talk to, but were afraid to. While others believed they weren't smart enough, or didn't have the credentials or self-esteem to talk to these people, he would make bold requests to spend time with them.

One day, he told me, there was one particular person he wanted to meet. The well-known investor lived in a small town. So, my friend did what nobody had ever thought of doing. He made a **bold** move. He booked a flight to the investor's hometown and called the guy up. He told him that he was in town, and wondered if he'd be open to going to breakfast. The guy was delighted. He said people typically didn't come to his hometown and he'd love to meet.

Reggie would end up making **bold** requests, like the example above, until he became one of the top real estate investors in the United States.

You don't know the outcome until you ask. Typically, the gold you're seeking is in the **BOLD** questions people dare to ask. Be bold in your requests.

Why?

Because nobody else is doing it. Stand out and ask the questions from a place of curiosity and drive, without any expectations.

My coach, Rich Litvin, told me that I could get as many clients as I wanted by collecting as many NO's as I could in one day. What if I had to collect 30 NO's today? Just go and ask people if they want coaching, if they want to hear what I do, have an hour to speak about their business, spend 10 minutes to tell me about their family life. What would happen if I didn't care about the outcome? What would that do to change my life? If boldness with a heart for serving was your only job, how far could you go in your coaching?

The best businessmen, the best coaches, and the best at anything make **bold** requests. They stand out because everyone else is in the noise of the ordinary. The bold dance to a different tune, and once others see that, they have no choice but to listen. It's a new song they're dancing to. It's never been done.

People love **bold** requests. Especially powerful people. Powerful people are used to having "pleasers" around them because they have money, fame, and success. Go to them with a **bold** request. They will love you for it. Tell them you have something that can change their life if they are willing to hear it. Tell them something nobody else will tell them in their life because they are afraid of the consequences. Tell them that you charge twice the amount, even five times the amount, of other coaches.

When they ask why...

You say because you ask the **BOLD** questions nobody else

dares to ask.

But...you have to ask them.

You have to be **BOLD**.

Show up with a **BOLD** question and have them look you square in the face and answer it.

Most all my clients I have coached appreciate the **BOLD** questions; the ones that show them a new world, the ones that break their barrier of normalcy.

Close this book right now and get 10 NO's by the end of the day. Invite people to a coaching conversation. Invite them to tell you their biggest dream; their biggest fears.

Make **bold** requests and don't be afraid.

Your world will change.

If you "had" to get someone to say NO to you every day for the next 30 days—what would happen?

— Rich Litvin

Chapter 18
Don't Charge By The Hour

After a certain point, money is meaningless. It ceases to be the goal. The game is what counts.
Aristotle Onassis

I used to be a hypnotherapist. I would charge by the hour. I moved over to become a coach with the same idea of charging by the hour. It was a terrible mistake. A huge one.

As a coach, my magic wasn't in the hour my clients spent with me. One insight from my coaching can make my client's business a million dollars. One insight can make 10 years of a failed marriage a success overnight. One insight can make what looked like a money struggle look like a fun problem for two minds to tackle. It could take an hour or it can take five minutes.

I don't charge by the hour anymore. The insights we can gain are too powerful to restrict to an arbitrary time limit. When you charge by the hour, you are now bound by the rule you've created. You have an hour to do the coaching dance, you're looking at your clock, and you're waiting in hopes your client will get some sort of shift.

I don't have that worry, nor do I ever want to be in that position. I charge by getting rid of their biggest fears and helping them achieve their dreams. Then, I dig deeper and see how long I'd like to work with the person in front of me to get them to this extraordinary, new place they have never ventured to before.

How much would you pay for someone to be a part of your biggest dream and get you closer to it? A lot more than coaches who are spending their time by the hour.

I work on dreams, not on time. Once the dream has been

established, you can figure out how long you'd like to spend working with the client; how long you see fit to see a transformation. I work with clients for a minimum of three months, and up to one year. In those three months, my clients can email me, call me (this doesn't mean they have access to me immediately) or set up laser coaching sessions.

I don't have to worry about my client clocking in. I can focus on getting them closer to their dreams. It doesn't suit me to work by the hour.

If you are reading this and you are doing just fine charging by the hour, then you don't have to worry about it. You're the coach; they're your rules.

If you are wondering what works for me and some of the most prominent coaches I've seen, they are more concerned about extraordinary results, and less concerned about the hours.

I don't charge by the hour. My clients' dreams are bigger than that.

Chapter 19
Money Isn't The Only Thing You'll Be Investing

I have no idols. I admire work, dedication and competence.
Ayrton Senna

As a coach you are going to have resistance. You are going to have clients tell you that they don't have the time right now to invest in coaching. You are going to have clients tell you that your fees are five times higher than any other coach they've worked with. You are going to have clients who are going to be indecisive. What are you supposed to do?

When I first started, a "NO" was scary. If I got a "NO," it hurt my self-esteem, my pride, and my sense of value. Now I realize that a "NO" simply means they don't see the value of what you are proposing to them. It's a wonderful gauge; a verbal barometer of where the conversation is straying. It has nothing to do with your self-esteem anymore than if you refuse a dessert at a restaurant.

If a server offers you coffee or dessert and you say "NO," this has no relevance to how you feel about the server. It has everything to do with someone giving you an answer to your request. And an answer is a perfect place to be in a dialogue.

People are afraid of "NO." People are afraid of the questions of affordability, whether they should be coached by you, or any questions that are prolonging the potential client from signing up.

Not for me.

The longer I stay in the "NO," the more committed a client I will have if they choose to work with me. What do I do when I get clients who tell me they can't afford it? I do what my coach Rich Litvin told me. Be the coach. Move it away from the money and back to their dreams. I love that. It works.

When a potential client is telling you that they may not be able to afford it, don't disagree with them. Dance with their answer and move it back to a place of a powerful conversation. Reverse the conversation so you are not cornered; where you are not explaining the reasons you are worth it. Agree with them and add to their conversation.

What if, instead of telling them, "Well, yeah, it can be expensive. Let me see if I can discount the fee or lower it for you because I really want to work with you..." you agree with them and reverse the role so now not only are you agreeing with them, you are making the stakes even higher.

What if you told them in the conversation, "You are absolutely correct; your financial investment for coaching is going to be a very high-level investment. And money will not be the only thing you'll be investing; you'll also be investing your time, your energy, and your commitment to be closer than you have ever been to achieving your high-level dreams. When you are ready to invest in this type of high-flame commitment, I'll be here to support you 100%."

Wait for your client to respond. Hold on to the strength of silence. That changes everything. What looked like a weak position is actually a powerful position to be in. A "NO" allows you to see where you stand in a conversation. A "NO" can make a coaching commitment solid. You want to have the "NO's."

The stronger the "NO's" the stronger the client will be in their commitments when they hire you. Your potential clients want a coach that can handle "NO's." They want to see what a coach will do when cornered, and in a place that may seem vulnerable.

Hope for these moments, because how you show up in these

moments...that's the person they want to coach them when they are at their weakest.

Rise above the "NO's" and challenge them. Reverse the role so you can let them know that you aren't afraid of "NO's" and that you don't play in "negotiating" on weak terms. You are hired to challenge them to rise above what they have been living with. You don't want to go into the world that they want to escape and elevate from. Their uncertainty is what has them stuck in their rut. So, why would you negotiate the terms of your coaching based on their uncertainty?

What if you asked your client, "I haven't heard from you and I was wondering what happened?"

Your client replies, "I know I could really use coaching in my business, but I am unsure if I can commit to it right now."

Your response: "What if I told you that this same uncertainty is the reason you cannot get out of the very same thing you want resolution for? You are looking for certainty and clarity in your business, family life, etc., but you are using the same mechanism, uncertainty, which hasn't allowed you to get what you want or to make a clear decision. What if we tackle this uncertainty and see where it leads?"

Uncertainty is a perfect place for a potential client to be. This allows you to show them the power of coaching and get rid of their uncertainty. Show them the power of taking action. Then they will see the power in you as a coach.

A weak coach would say, "Oh well, maybe when you get certainty...not sure when...but when you do, you can call me again."

Can you see how impotent that sounds?

You are a coach; a powerful one. Lead them to a powerful, action-based solution. They are looking for guidance and they just opened the door for you to show them a clear, powerful path they didn't know existed.

This is the power of role reversal.

Reverse the role so you aren't "defending" your position, but rather are opening up a powerful dialogue. Welcome the "NO" and change their world.

Chapter 20
Be A Brain Surgeon

Until you value yourself, you won't value your time. Until you value your time, you will not do anything with it.
M. Scott Peck

I have to admit, I am a sucker for coaching. I love coaching. I love seeing people's lives change in a matter of minutes. There is a double-edged sword to being a powerful coach. People will start to see that you are changing lives. People will be curious about what conversation a client had with you that shifted your client's way of thinking.

I would have a speaking engagement and as soon as I stepped off the stage, people would come to me for advice. I figured that since they didn't have much time and it's a nice thing to do, I would spend time with each person trying to give them a piece of my advice.

I'm getting embarrassed as I write this. As I write this, I realize how many of my friends asked me for "coaching" when all I was doing was being a sounding board for them to vent. There I was, thinking I was coaching, and there was no shift, no real direction to the conversation.

It was happening with friends, referrals, and people I would meet at someone's house or after a speaking gig. I didn't treat my profession with the value that it's worth. I remember asking my friend, who is a brain surgeon, about migraines. I told him that my girlfriend at the time, who was in the other room, was getting really bad migraines. I asked him if he'd like to speak to her. I was just curious.

He said, "Now is not the time, but I'd love to see if I could help."

He requested that I call his office and set up an appointment. Why? Because he valued his profession. He was a professional. It ended up that my girlfriend at the time never called him. Had the brain surgeon jumped to see what was going on, he would have wasted his time with someone who wasn't committed to finding out about her migraines.

So many coaches have clients who have "migraine" problems and aren't really committed to changing. I have realized in my coaching profession that the easiest way to weed out small talk and chatter is for someone to set up a time to have a powerful conversation. No small talk. It doesn't matter if it's your friend, a referral, or someone you've just met at a gathering. Be professional. Set up the right time and treat their time with you professionally. Make yourself a highly valued coach. Become a brain surgeon and don't "peek" to see what's going on. Set up the appropriate time to move them to a place they didn't think was possible.

Having small talk and telling whomever you're talking to that you are available at any moment is not starting the conversation in a powerful way. I only go to doctors who value their time—the ones who respect their professional time as well as their social time. I value doctors who see that their assistance could be beneficial, then take the time to see me in their office. That's where a doctor can do his magic. That's where he can commit 100% of his time to you.

Be like a brain surgeon. Your job as a coach is that important.

I have **RULES:**

✅ **I Coach KINGS & QUEENS:** I don't coach victims or people who believe that things happen to them. I am very selective with who I coach. If you believe you are in charge of your life and in charge of the changes in your life, I CAN COACH YOU.

✅ **I DO NOT USE TEMPLATES OR TECHNIQUES:** I work with you and I am devoted to what you need, not what I have read in a book or in my classes. My style of coaching is not for everyone. But anyone that is ready to be coached will make big changes in their relationships, business, and personal life.

✅ **YOU WILL BE VULNERABLE:** And I will also be vulnerable. I cannot coach a client that is not in the room; either physically, mentally, or emotionally. I expect my client to be transparent, REAL, and authentic. If I see that you are playing games or being inauthentic and you don't want to be coached, I will end the session with no refunds.

✅ **My number one priority is to be present with my client.** I don't care how much money you make, your title or your profession. You will strip away all of your ideas about yourself and be in the room with just me. You will also know that I will be just as real and authentic as you will be with me. This is my promise.

✅ **A Coach for Cheap is a CHEAP COACH.** I charge more than other coaches. I might be too expensive for you. The money you will invest with me will pay you back more than the session.

When you are ready to be WORLD CLASS, Click HERE.

www.amirkarkouti.com

79

He who does not understand your silence will probably not understand your words.
— Elbert Hubbard

Chapter 21
Powerful Coaching In Silence

Sitting silently,
doing nothing,
the spring comes
and the grass grows by itself.
Buddha

You may have heard the aphorism, "Don't just stand there—do something!" Buddha saw it a different way. He would say, "Don't just do something—stand there!" Buddha was onto something. He knew the power of standing or sitting silently. He knew that when you sit in utter silence, unmoved, undisturbed, not engaging in your restless thoughts, but just sitting and listening, doing nothing, the spring comes and the grass grows by itself. In other words, things happen even when you sit in silence and listen. As a matter of fact, I've found that in deep, powerful coaching, silence is the biggest ally to having breakthroughs.

I remember having a powerful, life-changing conversation about fundraising with my coach Rich. I was floored. He gave me insights I thought I could never get on my own. Later, when I went back to listen to the coaching call, I couldn't believe what I heard. Rich had only asked three questions in the two-hour conversation we'd had. The rest of the time he listened. He removed himself from being the doer of the coaching. His silence was not inactive; it caused great action through him without him being a doer.

I could tell he was hearing me and the connection to my own voice and thoughts became louder. I would talk out loud and sit.

Out of nowhere, a new thought would arise that gave way to the answers I was looking for. My coach just listened. There was a point where the silence became uncomfortable. He didn't care. Once I stopped caring, new insights arose.

Like the grass that grows when you're sitting in silence, insights, wisdom, and clarity arise from your clients when you sit in silence. If you want to be a powerful coach, deep listening is one of your most valuable assets.

What is deep listening? It's a way of *hearing* where our whole body and being are, in the moment, without controlling it, judging it, or changing anything. It's letting whatever will happen, happen in the conversation without jumping in. There is no need to clarify anything until you've sat in silence and your client is empty of words. Most of the time your client will clarify what's missing before you step in. That's more powerful than you telling them what needs to be done.

Why?

Because there is no need to convince your client when your client came up with the insight on their own. You have to open up space for them to come to their own conclusions, in deep silence. When you sit with your client, be open, alert, attentive, and receptive. It's a process where you have to be alert. It's not passive, like you're tuned out. You need to be aware of the whole person in front of you.

Don't listen with the idea of formulating a question while they speak. Come from a completely empty place. Trust that when the conversation is done, the question that needs to be said will arise. Until there is silence, no question is adequate.

You will know whether your silence is authentic or forced. When your silence is forced, it is not spontaneous. You can feel it. You will notice that you are ready to jump into the conversation and say your piece. When your silence is forced, you will feel the inner turmoil. It will feel distressing and you'll want to remove the silence. The words coming from your client are coming *at you* and not *through you* when your silence is forced.

As Sylvia Boorstein wrote: "You might think of the difference between radar that goes out looking for something and a satellite dish with a wide range of pickup capacity that just sits in the backyard, waiting. Be a satellite dish. Stay turned on, but just wait."

There is all the time in the world. Get used to sitting in silence. If there is nothing to be said, don't say it. What needs to be said will show up in the moment.

But why is it so hard to do? Because we are afraid of silence. We are not used to it. It's foreign to us. We are used to our automatic bias of *how does what they are saying affect me?* What can I say next to make this a better conversation? We interrupt, and we come to conclusions before the person can finish the sentence.

Our culture loves downloading information. We hear someone talk and we are either regurgitating information or are ready to debate and set someone straight. We can't hear between the lines; we just hear the surface of the conversation. We are not whole-heartedly listening. We are surface hearing.

Deep listening, sitting in silence, is so foreign to us that we have removed it from our existence. Yet, that's exactly what brings about breakthroughs and insights. Deep listening brings forth your intuition and gut feelings. It connects you to the moment. You become sensitive to all facets of your experience with the person in front of you—internal, external, and contextual.

I have signed up clients by asking one question and letting the person on the other line talk for an hour. One question. How many people in your life will let you talk for even a half an hour and allow you the space to make the shifts you want in a safe and quiet environment? Not many. Everyone always has something to say.

Not you. Sit in silence and see what happens. Clear a space to allow you to be open to receptivity. Notice your thoughts passing through, but don't care about them. Listen to your breathing and relax. Become aware of your body and become in tune with your senses. It will become second nature after some time. It's like riding a bike. After a while, you are steering, pedaling, and directing without knowing it.

Don't grasp at the sounds. Don't reject or interfere with the words. If there are no sounds, no conversation, listen and sit in silence. No more projecting your opinions, ideas, or defending yourself or your agenda. Deep listening challenges the way we engage in a conversation. Deep listening allows the person in front of you to trust that what they are saying, regardless of how well or poorly said, is coming from what's true in their heart and experience. They will feel that you're connected to what they are saying. The conversation will go above the words. The listening will go beyond our ears and eyes and come through our hearts and souls.

This allows for space in our heads for wisdom. It allows us to be a receptor for the person in front of us. It allows you to be selfless and removed from being self-centered. Because...it's not about you. It's about the person in front of you.

Rumi the poet once said, "Silence is the language of God, all else is poor translation."

I know what that means now. When I sit with my clients, I sit in silence and listen deeply. I now know the gifts and power of sitting and listening. What if, with your next client, you sat in silence and listened? Listened so deeply, like nobody has ever done in their life? What kind of transformation might occur that we weren't able to see before?

There is only one way to find out...

Most people do not listen with the intent to understand.
They listen with the intent to reply.

Chapter 22
You Are Not Your Credentials

*All credibility, all good conscience, all evidence of truth come only
from the senses.*
Friedrich Nietzsche

As I write this, I am feeling my own heat. I am 34 years old, and I don't have a college degree. With my brother's help, we bankrupted a very profitable business, lost our house, I had to sell my car, and start from scratch. So, who am I to coach others?

I am feeling my own heat because when people would ask me about my credentials, I used to be afraid. I didn't have credentials. At least, not the credentials that I thought were important in my own head. I thought when a potential client asked for credentials they were asking about where I went to college, how rich I was, and what certificates I had on my wall.

That's not what clients are asking when they ask for your credentials. They are asking in a roundabout way...How can you help me? That's it. They haven't had the opportunity to see the power of your coaching, so they are assuming that your "credentials" will shed some light.

Steve Chandler, another powerful coach, when asked what his credentials are, tells people that he was an alcoholic, had a failed marriage, and lost all of his money. When asked, "If those are your credentials, then how can you help us?" He replies, "Oh, you didn't ask me if I could help you, you asked me what my credentials are. The only way to find out if I can help you is to have a conversation."

I love that! He said he's told Fortune 500 companies that

answer and he's been hired.

Why?

Because they don't care about your credentials. They want to know that you can help them. Period. That changed the way I looked at credentials.

I change people's lives by talking to them; by opening a space for a miracle to happen. This has nothing to do with my credentials. My credentials, or lack thereof, have nothing to do with my success. I was so busy worrying about credentials that I stopped myself from going to businesses that I knew I could help. I would be so afraid of talking to someone who had more money than me, more education, or more "credentials" that I neglected to give the person in front of me 100% of my attention.

Why?

Because I was in my head, wondering when they would ask for my credentials. The truth is, if you serve the person in front of you powerfully, they don't care about your credentials.

Steve had an awesome story about coaching. At a seminar of his, he had us imagine a scene. We are in a desert and we have water. The people in the town are dying of thirst. The problem is, you are afraid to offer them water.

Why?

Well, what if they ask you about your credentials? What would happen then? NOTHING would happen. They would say, "To hell with your credentials, give us water!"

You have the water. You are the coach. Stop holding on to the water because you've made up some make-believe value of your credentials. Serve the people who can benefit from what you have to offer. Give them the gift of your coaching.

People are thirsty. Give them what they want. Don't stop yourself with this façade of credentials that is irrelevant to you being able to transform lives.

Go to businesses and give them a talk about productivity. Go to a nonprofit and increase their revenues. Go to high schools and talk to the students and staff about being extraordinary. When they ask you about your credentials, tell them that you change people's lives, and the only way to find out what you can do for them is for them to spend time with you.

You have to really believe that changing lives is possible. Call up businesses that can benefit from your services. Then show them what you can do. Change their business *before* they work with you. Show them the types of things they can do to improve their business *before* you leave the conversation.

Don't *tell* them. Don't tell them that you can help them or that you are amazing. Nobody cares. *Show* them how you can be amazing for their business *right now*. Get out of *telling* people what you do. If you start to tell them, then you're going to have to tell them your credentials.

I show up so powerfully in people's businesses that there is no time or place to have that type of conversation. I'm too busy shifting their minds. I am showing businesses ways to increase their income by the end of the working day. I am showing non-profits how to get donors to offer them money without marketing.

I am going to schools, sharing my challenges and struggles, and offering them ways to get out of their situations. I am going to the Chambers of Commerce and showing them how I got out of my debt, and setting up seminars to show their clients how to do it themselves...all before they have even hired me. You can do that, too.

People are thirsty and you have the water. Serve people your water and you will never have to worry about acquiring clients.

On Leaving a Legacy:

Every step you take is a footprint to your legacy. Your legacy is what you leave behind; that starts in this exact moment.
— Amir Karkouti

Chapter 23
Life Is An Infinite Game

Omnipotence is not knowing how everything is done; it's just doing it.
Alan Watts

I left this for the last chapter because secretly this is what makes the whole coaching business fun and interesting. As a matter of fact, this makes all aspects of life fun and worth pursuing.

I remember during one of my last phone calls with Rich I told him that I love doing what I am doing because I feel like I'm playing a game instead of "going to a job." For years, trying to get a client, and hearing them give me the reasons why they didn't need a coach, want one, or care for one, became exhausting. I would feel exhausted because I thought it had to do with my self-esteem, my value as a coach, and it was all about me.

When it's all about you and what you think your job, business, relationships, and everything else should look like in your life, you're missing a big part of the equation. You are turning your coaching into a chore—a thing that needs to be done.

Nobody likes to do chores. Nobody likes to be at a job where they're constantly being criticized. Yet, there I was, being my own worst critic. And the worst part of being the worst self-critic is I was with myself 24 hours a day. So, I couldn't escape this annoying, self-critical boss, even if I wanted to.

As I slowly got into the rhythm of enjoying all the aspects of coaching—the "NO's," the bold requests, the mess-ups, and the total embarrassments—all of a sudden the "bad" parts of coaching were just as exhilarating as the "good" parts.

It became a game. As I was explaining this newfound energy of waking up each morning and playing a game, Rich added a distinction that made the game even more amazing.

As I was talking to Rich, telling him about my experiences, he added, "Life is not only a game, it's an infinite game. It's an infinite game because you can change the rules at any minute. You can start again right this second. When life is an infinite game, you can't lose by design."

He was right. That's how I felt and he put it into words. So, I am here to finish off my book with a few requests.

I request that you coach today and make the biggest mess-ups, mistakes, and embarrassments you've ever made, with the total commitment of serving your client 100%. Knowing that you're in a game with infinite possibilities, this type of commitment might just be the starting point to being the coach no other coaches dare compare themselves to.

I request that when people ask you what you do, you do not squirm and come up with a clever sales pitch, but look them directly in the eye and tell them that you have conversations with people and you change their lives. If this doesn't resonate with you, then come up with something that moves you from your soul when you speak it.

Remember, you have infinite possibilities to share how impactful you are. Yet, so many coaches don't step into that space and resort to crawling back into their skin in hopes of not sounding "politically correct," or afraid that people won't believe them.

I request that you stop telling people what you do and SHOW THEM. Invite them to a two-hour conversation with you and go deeper than you have ever gone. Open yourself up, be vulnerable, be bold, and don't expect an outcome. Just expect to be present throughout the whole conversation. A powerful outcome will be the side-effect of being right next to them and creating that space of exploration, 100% attentive and present.

Last but not least, have fun. Go out there and during the worst days of your life, have fun. Know that you are in an infinite game, and play. I learned that from my coaches while I was going through a bankruptcy, and it changed my life. I am so glad that I learned early on in my life that events happening in my world have no direct correlation to me having fun.

I realized that for many, the reason going through a financial crisis, a break-up, or anything else, seems more horrendous than it needs to be is because they took the fun out of it.

I request that you make every disaster a project, a game, and a way to see it as something that will make you stronger, bolder, and more resilient. I request that you thank God, or whomever you want, for giving you more problems to solve in your life. I want you to know that in any game, the tougher the opponent the stronger your team will be. Search for tougher opponents, tougher times, and use your strengths to carry you over to be better.

Take one step forward and two steps back. For many that's a disaster; for me it's the cha-cha...a dance that is part of my life. After all, if life looks like it can't get any worse...remember, you can stop feeling that way right now and change the game... *infinitely*.

You owe it to yourself and to your extraordinary clients.

RESOURCES

I would not be here today if it weren't for the people in my life who pushed me beyond my own boundaries and had me make a shift in my thinking.

Here are some of the resources that I highly recommend to help get you further in your own coaching practice.

First and foremost, the person who was the biggest catalyst to transforming my coaching practice is my coach, Rich Litvin. I cannot thank him enough for all that he shared with me. Because of his deep questions and not letting me buy into my own stories, the transformations in all aspects of my life increased exponentially. Being coached by him is one of those life-changing experiences.

If for some reason you do not have the opportunity to be coached by him, he has awesome resources to move you along your coaching journey.

Rich Litvin:

Book:
The Prosperous Coach – Singlehandedly the best book on how to get high-paying clients and how to have a powerful coaching practice.

Website:
www.Richlitvin.com
theprosperouscoach.com

Steve Chandler

Steve Chandler has also been very instrumental in my journey to become a powerful coach. Although I have never been personally coached by him, I have seen him create miracles in front of me at the many seminars and events I have attended.

His books and audios are very powerful. I highly recommend any of the materials that are out there from Steve.

Books:
Wealth Warrior
Time Warrior
The Coaching Connection
Fearless
Relationshift

Website:
stevechandler.com
imindshift.com

I am a part of his Wealth Warrior movement and I highly recommend that any high-level coach be a part of it. You can check out the Wealth Warrior movement on his website.

Michael Neill

Michael Neill is one of the top coaches in the world. He has thousands of subscribers who listen to his weekly radio program and he is one of the most transformative coaches alive today.

I love watching Michael Neill coach. The simplicity and artistry in his coaching is like no other. He has a coaching academy with some of the leading coaches teaching the courses. You can find out more about Supercoach Academy at www.supercoach.com

Book:
The Inside Out Revolution

Website:
Supercoach.com

Jamie Smart

I've been following Jamie Smart for over 10 years. Since his days as an NLP trainer to his newest program called Innate Thinking®, he is on the cutting edge of coaching and transformative work.

Book:
Clarity

Website:
Jamiesmart.com

Steve Linder

Whether you want to increase your business, understand human psychology, or just elevate your game, Steve Linder's programs are an amazing resource. Although I have moved away from Traditional NLP, many of his teachings still resonate with me and I'd highly recommend any of his products or seminars.

Website:

Sriuniversity.com

Jeff Paro and Roberto Monaco

Jeff and Roberto were the first people to show me the power of transformational coaching. I was deathly afraid of public speaking. Through their extensive training for speakers, they showed me how to remove my psychological barriers and limiting beliefs. To go from being afraid to speak to looking forward to getting on stage, there is no better proof that powerful coaching works. I highly recommend their training.

Website:

influenceology.com

Of course, if you'd like to know more about what I do,
you can visit my site at:

www.amirkarkouti.com

To Your Success!

ACKNOWLEDGMENTS

The number of people in my life who have shaped me into the coach I am today could fill a book. I will try to make this as short as possible, knowing I will be missing many who helped make this book possible.

First and foremost, I'd like to thank Marilyn Rodriguez, an amazing woman and coach who sifted through my book and added her wisdom, which made this book the powerful book I envisioned it to be. Her constant questions and suggestions gave my book a newfound energy. Thank you for being a big part of this project. If you want a transformation from a powerful coach, you can reach her at www.themarilynrodriguez.com.

A BIG thank you to Randy Stuart, for his creative ideas with the cover design of my book. Looking forward to see what you plan to do with your creativity coaching.

I'd like to thank Reggie Lal. He was my "original" business coach and mentor. When I was going through losing everything—my business, my house, and my dignity—he showed me that you can either spend time wondering why this is happening to you, or take the smallest action toward getting your life back. He taught me to take immediate action, be bold in getting my finances back in order, and have fun doing it along the way. Instead of looking at what I was going through as a problem, working with Reggie made a problem into a fun project. I will be forever grateful for that.

Thanks to Craig Jacobson. Craig was just as instrumental in

helping me move to financial freedom. Craig is a small business advisor who showed me what's actually important in business— your customers and being able to communicate with them. When the economy tanked, I sought his expertise and overnight he created a plan that made us the #1 go-to restaurant in San Diego. (I own a few businesses, restaurants being one of them). When someone cares less about your problems than you do, a small business coach can exponentially grow your business because he's not in your "mess." Thank you for not playing into my "mess" and for being patient enough until we saw it for ourselves. You can visit his site at openspacesmarketing.com.

Thanks also to Reza Karkouti. Reza is my brother, business partner, and ultimate "client." I'd like to thank my brother for allowing me to test out all my coaching skills on him and our business. Some of my coaching ideas were extreme failures; but at least we know we are stuck with each other. That's what families are for. ☺

Special thanks to Jay Noblezada for bouncing ideas back and forth with me.

Thanks to my client and friend James Cappelman, who continues to inspire me and others through his real estate coaching program.

A very special thanks to my editor, Cris Wanzer, for ripping my book apart in a loving manner so everyone reading it can understand what I am trying to express. There are very few people in the world who can translate my thoughts so they make sense, and she happens to be one of them.

A final thanks to all my clients and people along the way that made this book possible. Everyone in my life—you have a piece of inspiration stamped in this book.